John Bascom

The New Theology

John Bascom

The New Theology

ISBN/EAN: 9783744651974

Printed in Europe, USA, Canada, Australia, Japan

Cover: Foto ©Lupo / pixelio.de

More available books at **www.hansebooks.com**

BY THE SAME AUTHOR.

I. ÆSTHETICS; OR, THE SCIENCE OF BEAUTY. 8vo, cloth.... $1.50
II. ETHICS; OR, THE SCIENCE OF DUTY. 8vo, cloth.......... 1.75
III. NATURAL THEOLOGY. 8vo, cloth....................... 1.50
IV. THE SCIENCE OF MIND. 8vo, cloth.................... 2.00
V. THE PHILOSOPHY OF ENGLISH LITERATURE. Lectures delivered before the Lowell Institute, Boston. 8vo, cloth.... 1.50
VI. THE GROWTH AND GRADES OF INTELLIGENCE; OR, COMPARATIVE PSYCHOLOGY. 8vo, cloth.................... 1.50
VII. A PHILOSOPHY OF RELIGION; OR, THE RATIONAL GROUNDS OF RELIGIOUS BELIEF. 8vo, cloth..................... 2.00
VIII. PHILOSOPHY OF RHETORIC. 8vo, cloth................. 1.25
IX. THE WORDS OF CHRIST. 8vo, cloth.................... 1.50
X. PROBLEMS IN PHILOSOPHY. 8vo, cloth................. 1.50
XI. SOCIOLOGY. 8vo, cloth............................... 1.50

G. P. PUTNAM'S SONS,   New York and London.

BY

JOHN BASCOM

AUTHOR OF "A PHILOSOPHY OF RELIGION; OR, THE RATIONAL GROUNDS
OF RELIGIOUS BELIEF," "THE WORDS OF CHRIST AS
PRINCIPLES OF PERSONAL AND SOCIAL
GROWTH," ETC., ETC.

G. P. PUTNAM'S SONS

NEW YORK   LONDON
27 WEST TWENTY-THIRD ST.   27 KING WILLIAM ST., STRAND

The Knickerbocker Press

1891

THIS VOLUME IS INSCRIBED TO

EDWARD ORTON,

WHOM I FIRST LEARNED TO LOVE ON ANDOVER HILL
—A POINT OF REVOLUTION AND DEPARTURE
FOR US BOTH

CONTENTS.

CHAPTER	PAGE
Preface	vii
Introduction	1
I.—Naturalism	11
II.—The Supernatural	73
III.—Dogmatism	113
IV.—Pietism	157
V.—Spiritualism	188

PREFACE.

THIS work is equally removed in its conclusions from the opinions of those who think that, in the deeper questions of being, we can know nothing, and waste our time by inquiry; and the opinions of those who suppose that we are already sufficiently instructed in these directions by revelation, and have only to hold fast its truths. It proceeds on the supposition that there is truth of infinite moment attainable by man both from nature and from revelation, both from the constitution of the world and from the aggregate of human experience under it, but that this truth is of such breadth and magnitude that our measurements are all necessarily partial and ephemeral. A range of mountains is none the less visible, none the less inspiring, because we can see but a small portion of it from any one point, and because even this portion changes rapidly with a shifting of position or a transfer of light. It is this mobility of a vision that makes it divine.

Great things are, in the measure of their greatness, incomprehensible, yet our knowledge of them is of more worth than all other knowledge, is as truly knowledge as our knowing of the most minute and sensuous things.

We see by the light of a sun not one millionth part of whose rays ever enter the eye; we behold, in the spiritual world, by the light of truths which transcend our perception of them like the depths of infinity. Yet it is this very fact that distinguishes man from all the creatures near him. While he stands on great heights, he is intellectually filled with things far beyond his vision. He flings his life forward, and wins it again in the empty spaces of thought. He casts his bread on the waters, and gathers it after many days. He that saves his life by a prudent economy of inquiry loses it, and he that loses his life in the boldness of well-timed faith saves it; nowhere is a whole-souled venture more applicable than in the higher ranges of thought. We submit ourselves to nature, we submit ourselves to revelation; we are restrained here, and helped there; now sobered, and now quickened in inquiry, but all in obedience to the ends of life. This is the spirit of the work here offered; a trust in the powers of the mind—in many ways aided and corrected—laboriously, patiently, vigorously, to fulfil all the ends of thought. To ask a question, is to have a clue to the answer. We make no further apology for returning again to difficult discussions.

THE NEW THEOLOGY

INTRODUCTION.

THAT which is designated as the New Theology is, on the constructive side, the most general and conspicuous religious fact of our time, and by far the most significant one. What I have to say aims at a better understanding of this fact, in itself, in the forces which give rise to it, and in its practical results.

The New Theology is after all not a theology. There is no creed that we can call the new creed; there is no conclusion or series of conclusions that occupies, in this movement, any more a final position than do other allied convictions. The New Theology is not a creed but a tendency; is not a result but a movement. All men may feel it and share it,—most cultivated men do share it,—no man can make it his own or sufficiently voice it. Indeed it consists largely in breaking old bonds and in refusing to accept new ones. It is a ferment in the religious mind, an excitement in the religious camp, of which many marches are already the result, from which many more are to come. Some of these marches have carried those who have taken part in them quite beyond the lines of safety, and, as we think at least, over the uncertain borders which separate belief and unbelief. Such marching, because it is bold, even to recklessness, and is yet the result of the new inspiration, is not, therefore, its most complete or most just expression. Some have hardly left the camp, and only slightly shifted their quarters in it, yet this restlessness has the same cause and the same significance as the rashness of their fellows. The New Theology is to be judged by that which is sound, safe, and moderate in it, and not by its excesses or its insufficiencies.

The New Theology stands for an awakening in religious thought which leads it to seek for more flexible, less rigid; more productive, less barren; more living, less dead forms of expression and action, and by means of them to come fully under the progressive movement which belongs to our time as one of enlarged knowledge and renewed social life. One of the most conservative forms of thought is the religious form. But that conservatism has been sensibly reduced in many directions, and that fact is the fact of the New Theology,—the greatest fact in the history of the period because it expresses the utmost power and stretch of the tendencies that are securing change, that are pushing men onward, and bringing forward the Kingdom of Heaven.

The point of greatest interest in this movement is not what leading minds now think, but what directions, what degrees, what rapidity, of progress are to be occasioned by the pulsation of faith in the religious mind as a whole. Our only test of these later results is what we ourselves regard as the most guarded conclusions of the soundest thinkers of to-day, but we may be well assured that humanity, in traversing more slowly the same wilderness of thought, will not pitch its tents in exactly the same positions we have chosen, nor tarry in them merely because we have found it convenient to rest there.

The real question in society, in religion, even in philosophy, is the question of the masses. As the glacier, by its immense weight and untiring pressure in all directions, seeks out, and furrows out, through every zig-zag, the lowest lines of advance, so the popular mind, by the slowness, the multiplicity, the universality of its impressions, successfully unites the very facts of life with the very ideas which give them the safest and most comprehensive solution. If the movement is exceedingly slow, it is far less erratic than that of the more gifted. While much is due to rapidity, much is also due to inertia, in intellectual soundness; and we are interested in the New Theology not merely on account of the sudden accelerations of thought which overtake the minds of intellectual men by means of it, but because of the retardations and corrections and final resolutions it is suffering, and is to suffer, under popular sentiment. This sentiment as often expends itself indirectly, in social problems, as directly, in religious speculation. It brings to the solution of the theories of life the forces of life, and gives them that final, concrete exposition from which there is no escape. The social eagerness of the many is akin to the speculative interest of the few, and later results will combine them both.

We understand, then, by the New Theology a movement —one that is to be measured by masses, and often to be watched with most care at points at which it is the slowest. It is the essence of this movement that there is really nothing new in it, nothing final; that its features of interest, as in all progress, are direction, volume, rapidity, and that it has just now received a new name, because the slope of thought has made all these factors, for the moment, conspicuous.

The most obvious occasion for this accelerated movement in theology has been the progress of knowledge in other directions, more especially in science. This advance of knowledge has forced a reconstruction of the religious idea of the origin of the world, of the order and dependence of physical events, of the time occupied by them, and of the part they play in development. This revision of thought would have carried with it no great difficulty had not the dogmatic temper previously brought to these outlying questions a certainty and authority that do not belong to them. The fortune of central spiritual truths had come, in men's minds, to be identified with that of the remote conceptions associated with them, and so such a topic as that of the creation of the world raised the entire question of the adequacy and authority of religious instruction. The infallible is cut off from correction. Readjustment is impossible, and so great riffs, deep faults, began to appear in faith.

Science has also altered our conception of the government of God, and so somewhat of his character; the natural has gained immensely on the supernatural. A new statement of both of these forms of action is called for, and of their relation to each other. The confusion and the difficulty of thought at this point have been very great, and neither science, nor philosophy, nor religion, has been able to give us any generally accepted solution. Science, as interested in naturalism, and religion, as identified with supernaturalism, have inevitably slipped into conflict; the conflict which is incident to diverse and partial views, whose lines of reconciliation and union have not been found.

Just here a most thorough reconstruction of thought is called for—one that shall reach equally our physical and moral conceptions, our practical and spiritual experiences. Science has frequently fallen into a dogmatism at this point which has served to relieve the dogmatism of religion, and to make the contest between them somewhat more equal. Absolute naturalism in science is as untenable as easy-going supernaturalism in faith. The general mind will accept the latter as readily as the former, and is waiting for a philosophy that will accord as full a recognition to the laws of mind as to those of matter. Or rather it possesses latent within itself such a philosophy, and is looking for its more full exposition, defence, and acceptance. Nor does a positive assertion of agnosticism help the position of science. The human mind will not suffer itself to be curbed in pushing inquiries, which profoundly interest it, without an altogether sufficient reason. The giving of the reason opens anew the entire discussion.

An occasion for a profound movement in religious thought has been found in the inevitable extension of naturalism, incident to the progress of science, an extension almost as direct in its effects on religious ideas and methods of work as on invention and labor.

Science has also brought with it new methods of proof, has altered the relation between deduction and induction, and has led us to seek and to demand in all statements which touch facts, even remotely, the confirmation of experience. The facile ways of deduction are much narrowed, and many of the conclusions which have been made to rest upon them are received with incredulity. The exact conclusions concerning the subjective constitution of God, known as the doctrine of the Trinity, arising largely from verbal analysis, seem little better than moonshine, when contrasted with the faithful, flexible conceptions of science, won in the very presence of the facts to which they pertain. Hence there is present to us a new estimate of proof, and of the proper subjects of inquiry, and this brings with it a decisive change for the dogmatic and theological temper. In this movement there is some excess, unwarrantable depreciations, and unreasonable exaltations, of method, but, as a very profound and valid step of progress, it touches religious thought in many ways, and brings to it correction on many sides. The nature of dogmatism, and the limits of religious discussion, are thrown upon the mind for fresh consideration.

A still more important regenerative force has been found, in this passage from the old to the new, in ethical inquiry. The law of conduct in individual and social development, in national life, and in the historic progress of the race, is the latest and fullest fruit of knowledge. The ethical law, in its authority, and in the multiplicity of its applications, must ever grow in the minds of men. This law, demanding so much investigation, ever taking to itself new and higher services by virtue of the services already rendered, ever leading to more perfect insight by the insight already achieved—this law, shaping itself into fresh forms of the divine grace, demands constant reconciliation with religion, and a constant reconciliation of religious truth with it. The divine character, the fundamental principles of faith, find the record of facts in which, and by which, they are brought near to us, in the moral discipline and growth of the world; and the harmonizing of our religious conceptions with the facts to which they pertain in society must forever go forward by means of this inquiry into the laws of conduct.

Religious action that does not perpetually reshape itself to these laws of conduct, growing up under the increased insight and widest experience of men, becomes religiosity, checking the freedom of thought, and barring out the Kingdom of Heaven. The purity and power of faith at any one period or place must depend on its harmony with the forces of ethical construction there present. While religion corrects morality, morality equally corrects religion, and the two interlace each other as the form and force of the same thing. Indeed, if we accept the fact of the divine being and character as established, morality covers the laws of conduct which grow out of this fact, taken in connection with our own constitution, the constitution of society, and of the world to which we belong. Between sound religion and safe morals there is no distinction of subject-matter. They are both the interpretation of the same set of facts. The only way in which there springs up a difference between them is by a limitation of the facts accepted, or by a divided method of growth under them. If we deny the being of God, we destroy religion, but only weaken morality. Ethics takes its start in the character of man and his immediate social relations, and from this centre, under the growth of experience, lays down the laws of conduct. Religion starts with the character of God and the convictions of faith supported by revelation, and from this point of light declares the nature of righteousness and the rules of behavior. The results, in either case, should be the same. Our base lines lie in the same field, and our surveys should meet in identical measurements. No moral deductions from the character of God as to the government of the world should contradict the careful inductions of experience, gathered under that very government itself. Indeed, these two processes of thought are present for the very purpose of mutual correction, and any conflict between them implies error in one or in both.

Our piety must be morally sound and productive, and have the practical wisdom and extension of experience; and our morality must have the vigor of piety and its undying inspiration, if the two are to be constituents of sober character, outer and inner phases of a divine life. The love which is of God must express itself in a wide and wise culture, which nourishes human powers and affections through the entire field of individual and social growth.

There is a scepticism of unsatisfied feeling in our time that we have most of all to fear. It is a scepticism taking possession of the working classes, because they do not find the heart of Christ in the church of Christ. Socialism, in its inner force, is a mistaken search for a social construction which shall fulfil the second commandment, at least on its formal side. The masses crave the unity and strength which belong to the Christian idea; and if they turn from that idea, as expressed in the faith of our day, it is because the truth is not offered to them in a form in which they recognize it. We fall off from the wisdom of God in our dogmatic statements, and so provoke a scepticism of thought; we miss the love of Christ in social construction, and so call forth a wider, more dangerous, more revolutionary scepticism of the affections. It is in our hearts that we affirm there is or there is not a God. A sound moral sense, sustaining itself with the force and tenderness of the religious emotions, would win men back, in full ranks, to the Kingdom of Heaven. Our social problems are most urgently and directly the problems of faith.

The movement which we designate as the New Theology owes much of its vigor to a renewed effort to unite the pietism of religion and the virtue of morality to a higher, wider, deeper spiritualism, which shall have the mastery of ideas in their practical development, and by this practical development shall rise continually into purer and more just conceptions of them. This union of the present with the future, the life that now is with the life that ought to be; this meeting God in the works of God; this making revelation the light that lighteth every man that cometh into the world, are the substance of the New Theology; new only in casting aside the mischievous limitations of faith, and giving it free play once more in the work of interpretation, correction, and inspiration which falls to it. Faith that was ceasing to grow is planted in fresh soil, and becomes again the tree of life, bearing twelve manner of fruits, and yielding its fruit every month; while its leaves are for the healing of the nations.

The present volume proposes five topics of consideration, which closely concern the New Theology: Naturalism, Supernaturalism, Dogmatism, Pietism, and Spiritualism. The discussion will involve a partial reconsideration of topics before discussed by me, but the importance of the topics, their modified presentation and new relations, will justify this demand for fresh attention to them. While these topics of thought in their final statement are the most difficult that come before us, they return to us as no other topics do, and affect the inner flow of thought and outward form of action with a vigor all their own. As long as life is more than meat, will men consider, and be wise in considering, these themes which bring rest to the mind within itself, and lay down lines of thought and laws of conduct that stretch to the spiritual horizon. The mind raises questions for the very end of answering them, and though the answers may be long in coming, the inquiries themselves imply the movements of thought which are finally to bring them.

An agnosticism that raises doubts, and then professes an absolute inability to solve them, overlooks the fact, at least in part, that the push and pertinacity of inquiry arise from the clues that are leading to its resolution. We would stand by all that is given to knowledge and sound faith, both in matter and in mind, and put once more the same questions that men have put from the beginning, believing that while no answer is absolute, each succeeding answer may be more exact, more complete, than any preceding one. We may well remember that we are, where all men should love to be, at the dawn of reason. Though the day seems to break slowly into light, our impatience is the impatience of children who take slight measure of the events and processes about them. If we were to have more, we should in truth have less, having a weaker hold on the inner force of facts, dropping into a sensuous measure of things and out of the spiritual range of ideas.

CHAPTER I.

NATURALISM.

We understand by naturalism the universal presence of laws in the world, and their coherence in a complete system. We do not, however, understand by it one form of law, to the exclusion of other forms; but the union of different forms in one harmonious whole. Naturalism includes, therefore, not simply physical laws, but intellectual laws and moral laws as well; the laws of matter, of thought, and of conduct. It embraces not simply forces, but reasons and motives. It has to do not only with the coherence of causes and effects, but also with the connection of premises and conclusions, and the union of feelings and actions in volition. If we insist on naturalism under the single form of physical law, we shall soon, if we are coherent in our thinking, involve the spiritual world in a deadlock that cannot be overcome.

The world has unity, not identity, of method; coherence, not sameness, of parts. Naturalism means this unity and coherence, and because of it the system of things is wholly fitted to the reason of man. The element of reason in it is not fragmentary and sporadic, but concurrent and pervasive. To say this is only another way of asserting naturalism. The prevalence and power of reason in the world, by which it becomes the school of reason to man, constitutes its naturalism—the systematic presence of method. This naturalism is an essential condition to inquiry and to control, to knowledge and to conduct. Action which is not mechanical, nor organic, nor instinctive, but, higher than these, rational, must have a rational basis of procedure, and this basis is law. When law ceases, reason ceases; and action ceases as the expression of thought. All moral discipline must come to an end along those lines which divide order and confusion, an action of method and methodless action.

This truth of naturalism, though always present more or less to men's thoughts, is the one emphatic lesson of science; a lesson which has unspeakably enriched the human mind, increased its powers, and enlarged its responsibilities. In the enforcement of naturalism, science has found itself in conflict with religion, because religion has cherished many expectations, and adopted many methods, not well grounded in law; has conceived and entertained a supernatural more or less in conflict with the natural, and has thereby lost the secure footing of obedience to law, an obedience science never wearies of enforcing. Here is a discrepancy in our two methods of thought of utmost moment, and one to be overcome only by a thorough reconsideration of the religious notion of supernaturalism, on the one side, and a wise extension of the scientific idea of naturalism, on the other. Our first step toward this enlargement and harmony of thought is a reinforcement of the completeness and coherence of the divine method, a reassertion of naturalism as the basis of spiritual life equally with physical life. While naturalism must be redefined, it is a fatal mistake to carry our religious experience away from it. This is a leading occasion of the New Theology, and its primary result is the extended recognition of a comprehensive naturalism, covering both the physical and the spiritual, and rendering them a suitable field for the coherent, rational development of the powers of man. God and man thus meet, in one continuous, progressive, and prosperous movement. The divisions of the universe, if not healed, are being healed, by the grace of God. We are coming to understand all things as organic parts of one process—redemption.

In one direction, especially,—both because the inquiry is initiatory, and is a favorable example of method—we wish fully to enforce the strictly natural terms of faith, that of inspiration. We must know, to begin with, on what terms the mind deals with religious truths. The prevalent notion of inspiration, so far as it implies a supernatural and final authority in Revelation, takes the truths of Revelation from under the ordinary laws of thought, and enforces them upon the mind in a manner alien to the development of reason. So far as religious truth rests on authority, it ceases to rest on reason, ceases to be a discipline to reason, ceases to be subject to its laws. Reason may, and often must, accept much on authority, which it does not, for the time being, understand. This is no suspension of reason. Its earlier action is found in testing the sufficiency of the authority, and its later action in testing, at its leisure, the correctness of the assertions made under that authority. At neither point can reason be straitened without pushing the mind from its proper basis. The inquiry into the rightfulness of authority must usually precede the inquiry into the truth which the authority supports; but it can never suspend that inquiry when the proper time for it comes. The one act only prepares the way for the other. The length of time that may lapse between them is a matter of the mind's growth and of convenience.

The doctrine of inspiration, so far as it creates an authority external to the mind itself, and makes that authority final, slips from the basis of naturalism, and, at the very threshold of theology, separates religious truth from all other forms of truth, takes it from under the laws of mind to which it is addressed, and enforces it in a supernatural way. This method we believe to be profoundly unreasonable, since it arises in partial suspension of reason in its highest function; this method we believe to be profoundly unwise, since it tends to prevent the free, hearty, and sufficient exploration of this highest field of thought, thus enclosed by the quickset hedge of authority. The continuity of the intellectual and spiritual world is thus broken up, and we have a dividing line beyond which the powers of mind are in suspension. Of course, this suspension, so obviously inadmissible in itself, is enforced with many evasions and concessions; it should not be enforced at all. Every measure of arrest is a loss to the mind of its proper activity, and that, too, in the best and holiest direction. We may well pluck off our sandals when we tread holy places, but to tread them is the divine gift.

The works and words of God are not divided in their relation to mind. If the works of God can bear all the limitations, delays, and failures of reason, so can his words. If the works of God yield the largest service to man in calling forth inquiry and in responding to it, so do his words. If the works of God, direct from the hand of God, may still bear human handling, so may his words, which come to us through the mutable minds of men.

What is now to be said will be regarded by some as an attack on inspiration, and so an attack on religion. It is not an attack on inspiration, except as inspiration is enforced in suspension of the laws of the mind; nor on religion, except as religion is fenced about by a supernaturalism which disguises its true character. Religion rests on a divine method which penetrates the world from centre to circumference, a method which is the fulness of the divine thought. In this form we wish to possess it and defend it, and, therefore, we are willing to break down those barriers of authority, which, like the uncalled-for defences of a camp, take from us the true field of conflict.

We wish to see the Scriptures reposing on their own basis, the only sufficient and secure basis, of intrinsic truth; we wish to see them fully restored to all the uses— even abuses, if you please—of mind; we wish to acknowledge and possess an inspiration which consists in the soul's mastery of its own medium of life, its inbreathing of its own native air, the spiritual presence and love of God. There is a naturalism by which the physical world holds the wisdom of God like a saturated solution; by which the laws of thought are seen to have everywhere constructive mastery; by which the affections of the mind are offered to us as the last, highest, fullest product of growth—this naturalism, the way of God, and the way to God; this naturalism, the path of light that threads the creation from the beginning, passing ever more and more into perfect day, we are in search of, and must be allowed, no matter how dizzy the height or perilous the way, to pursue in humble, faithful exploration, helped, in spite of all apparent difficulties, by every inspired agent and servant of God.

In an attempt to establish naturalism as the only secure foundation of religious life, the methods of religious truth must first be settled. We must know, at the very outset, to what laws of inquiry we are committed, or whether to any laws; whether in the highest form of search into truth, the work is to be done for us, or whether we are to be trusted to it and it to us with that hesitancy, feebleness, and obscurity which fall to our powers; whether the power is helped or we are helped in the use of the power; whether truth is eternally truth in living action under its own laws, or whether it is capable of an unconscious transfer, and can be made to play an obscure, yet vital, part in a mind that is not mastering it.

We can meet with no great success in religious inquiry till we correctly understand our sources of knowledge and their right method of use. Evidently the existence, character, and government of God are to be established, if established at all, in connection with the constitution of the world, and pre-eminently in connection with its spiritual constitution. If these outer and inner facts of being do not contain and confirm our religious theory, that theory is void, for it is ultimately a theory of these very things. The world, then, in its physical, intellectual, social, and spiritual features offers the fundamental facts which we have occasion, in religious thought, to understand and expound.

A more familiar source, and, to most minds a more direct source, of religious truths is the Scriptures, what we term Revelation. It is of the utmost moment that we apprehend correctly the relation of Revelation to our empirical inquiries into the constitution of man and of society. These last are necessarily changeable and growing terms with us, and our new knowledge from these and kindred sources must either bring fresh interpretation to Revelation, or increasingly collide with it. The freedom, form, and force of our investigation in the field of actual life—spiritual life as we know it—will turn very much on our notion of the nature of this controlling term in religious thought, Revelation. Our view of it may be such as greatly to narrow inquiry, or such as greatly to enlarge it; such as to perplex its processes, or such as to accelerate them.

The character of Revelation is discussed as the doctrine of inspiration. Nothing, in our religious methods, will be more controlling than our conception of this doctrine. There are much vagueness and diversity of opinion on the topic, and yet there is a very general concurrence, in Christian churches, in the belief that inspiration stands, in some very peculiar way, for a divine word which is sufficient and final in religious thought; that Revelation takes the things disclosed by it out of the category of truths to be constantly investigated and forever restated, and puts them in that of truths to be apprehended and accepted once for all. The doctrine of inspiration thus goes far to determine the nature and limits of inquiry in the religious world. An authoritative rule of faith and practice is something very different from an open and changeable field of investigation.

No degree of labor, therefore, is lost which is directed, at the very outset, to this dependence on each other of natural and revealed religion, of the truths we are still reaching and those we have already reached. If these are so far removed from each other as to have different sources of authority, and to make different appeals to the human mind, we must have that fact constantly in view, and, even then, much perplexity will arise from it. This feeling of diversity is the more common religious experience, and gives occasion to a very conservative and dogmatic temper, and one distrustful of inquiry in the actual world. The office of religion is felt to be rather the creation of a new world, than the development of the world that now is.

We believe, and wish to show, that the two forms of truth are one and the same, rest on identical grounds, and must be unfolded concurrently. We wish to aid in opening all paths of thought. Inspiration is the mind's mastery of truth,—nothing less than this and there is nothing greater than this—and this mastery is in no person, at no period, and in no important particular, complete. The rational criteria of knowledge are uniform, throughout the realm of thought, no matter how purely spiritual that thought may be.

A doctrine of inspiration that affirms the divine authority of any principle, aside from the insight of the mind of the recipient, involves an inadmissible idea, is without sufficient proof, fails to perform the very service expected of it, and interferes, at every stage, with the just development of religious truth.

The idea is untenable in the degree in which we strive to give it distinctness. There are three kinds of truths in the Bible: those which contain fundamental principles in the divine government and in human conduct, those which utter the feelings of the writers in their own personal experience, and those which are simple statements of facts. It is in connection with the first form of truth, the truth of principles, that the doctrine of inspiration is of most moment. Some are ready to confine it to these spiritual truths, and yet, after all, it is least applicable to them. Insight alone gives us the mastery of the truth, and makes it truly valuable. In the measure in which principles are understood are they possessed, and in the measure in which they are obscure are they lost, by us.

Truths cannot be used successfully as mere rules of thumb in action. When we miss comprehension, we miss the point of light, the point of power. If, then, the last and highest phase of exaltation in religious truth transcends insight, we are putting darkness in place of light where light is most precious. We object to any view of inspiration which precludes error by overstepping the human mind, because it breaks down the inner organic force of thought in the very act in which God most strengthens it. It humbles us inexplicably, where God exalts us unspeakably. No life can come out of a process which itself lacks life, and least of all in the spiritual world. The soul never so lives, as when it lives before God in the light of his truth.

We must accept the freedom and force of the mind in grasping the truth, otherwise the truth is not grasped. The power of understanding the truth is of so critical and profound an order that it must be allowed to complete itself according to its own nature. Nor can we properly say that any comprehension of truth by a sacred writer is due to a foreign impulse. The normal as opposed to the abnormal, the natural as contrasted with the divine, is defined by the very fact that the percipient mind does, by its own free movement, enter into the truth as truth, and that to the very limit of its comprehension of it. It would not be more unphilosophical to say that the prophet, in a portion of his physical functions, lives by a miracle, than to say that he in part thinks by a miracle. Thought as thought is, in all its degrees, natural; as human thought, it is limited in all its degrees, and, in all its degrees, is open to variety, partiality, error. It can retain its constitution on no other terms. We have no occasion for two causes of one thing, and the one cause of human thought is the human mind, aided in many ways, but in no way overpowered, by the divine mind.

The advocates of an inspiration that fills human speech, as a dry conduit of words, with the living flow of divine thought, do not seem to have sufficiently considered the incompatibility of the two terms they are handling. Incongruous things are united by them in impossible ways. Language and idea can only coalesce as a living process of thought. This union must take place either in the human mind or in the divine mind; or the two must unite in and by the truth. The truth is the only point of spiritual contact. To put any strain upon our faculties beyond their own normal activity is so far to confound them; is to turn vision into illusion by pressure upon the eyeball. Nothing is more removed from all knowledge than words which have lost their interpretation within the mind itself. They are stones without cement—that leak at once the living waters that are entrusted to them. That which is understood affiliates with itself throughout under the action of the comprehending mind; it has no affiliation with that which is not understood.

Even in prophetic vision, it is something seen and felt, and so far understood, that is spread before the eye. The prophetic mind is prophetic because it catches the gleam of the winding river. The light of God's presence is on the years before it as on the years behind it. An inspiration that should exceed insight, and yet claim to be of the nature of truth, would be as unintelligible as if no human mind intervened, as if we saw unknown words suddenly appear upon the wall. We should have instant recourse to a teacher who could read and understand for us the inscription. It is astonishing, to the verge of foolishness, the way in which we speak of the truth, and bow to it, and salute it, as if it were an external reality, and not only and forever an inner, spiritual presence, born of our own thoughts. We are willing to turn the high-priest of truth into the keeper of a fetich, as if he were more to us thus than as ministering to the life of the soul within the soul itself— leaving us to make what way we can with the divine message.

There is no inspiration except in truth, and no truth except in the vision of the mind. Words do not contain it, but only words that are comprehended. That would be a strange revelation which revealed nothing, but the truth is revealed only as the mind is in living interplay with the vehicle of expression. We might as well regard light as disclosure independent of the eye, as to conceive the light of God's spiritual kingdom as a certain something transmissible without vision.

This brings us to another difficulty. If religious truth is given in an inspiration that transcends the powers of mind it should be, nay it must be, transmitted from person to person in a like way! How can the pupil perceive what the teacher could not conceive! How can we rise to truth the apostles could not win! In its daily uses the truth must settle at once to the level of the minds of those who have to do with it. Speaker and listener must stand on the same spiritual basis. In the degree in which truth rises above the moral level in which it is employed it is useless; it is no longer truth for any purpose of those interested in it. The spaces between the powers which can understand a principle, when it is stated, and the powers which can grasp that principle, in the facts which contain it, are only human spaces—spaces traversable by human thought. If we separate the mind of the teacher from the lesson he is to communicate by a stretch too great for his comprehension, he must necessarily cease to be a teacher. We acquire truth by coming in contact with a mind that has mastered it. If, therefore, in our theory of Revelation we put between the first message and the receiver of it an interval too great for the human mind, we have done either a mischievous thing or an unnecessary thing: unnecessary, if we are each of us to master the Revelation all the same ; most mischievous, if we are cut off from this mastery.

In the last analysis, what the doctrinaire affirms by inspiration is the inspiration of his own mind. No other inspiration can help him. His own mind is the sole medium of truth ; as his own eye is of vision. The doctrine he affirms to be unmistakable is his own conception of that doctrine. When Calhoun claimed the right of the citizens of South Carolina to carry their property, to wit, slaves, into the territories with the same freedom with which the citizens of Massachusetts carried their property, to wit, household goods, into them, Webster responded : "We hold our property under common law; you hold your property under the local law of South Carolina. What you are demanding to make universal is that law which is an abomination to mankind."

What the theologian wishes to carry with him as of universal authority is his own conception of truth. He has nothing else to offer. We are all agreed that truth in itself, truth yet to be disclosed, whether latent in nature or in Revelation, will have full, divine authority when it comes. All that we wish to secure is perfect freedom in mining, reducing, and coining this gold. We admit no pre-emption.

This difficulty and kindred difficulties have been obscurely felt, and have resulted in a constant reduction of the doctrine of inspiration, till only a shadow of its former self remains,—a subtile presence sustaining the mind in its spiritual action. Yet the only logical outcome of this softening tendency is naturalism, the mind free with its own powers. In the measure in which it lacks freedom, it lacks use, and the growth incident to use.

The simplest form of the doctrine of inspiration, as the communication of truth without error, is the earlier form of verbal dictation. This gave at least an exterior product of a definite kind. Yet such an inspiration is so wholly out of keeping with the circumstances of Scripture composition, so inconsistent with the changeable forms and hap-hazard ways in which the Word has come down to us, so opposed to the real wants of men as to make it rationally untenable—outside the possible conclusions of a sound judgment. It is new cloth in an old garment that instantly makes the rent worse. But between this view and the view that inspiration stands simply for the mind's hold upon truth, there is no intelligible stopping-place. The mind may be quickened and aided in many ways, it may attain penetrative and wide vision, but it cannot be pushed beyond its own limits, or be checked within them, without becoming confused, helpless, mechanical in its action. If its own insight is overstepped, something like verbal dictation must take the place of knowledge; if it is repressed in its own powers, something very like defeat and barrenness must follow. The divine may be enclosed in the human, and it is so enclosed in all just, spiritual thought; but how can it either restrain or transcend the human, without making the uses to which the human is then and there put to the same degree formal and valueless?

The surplus of revelation beyond insight, in whatever way it is given, cannot be truth, either to him who utters it or to those who receive it. It is the frenzy of an oracle the rhapsody of a mind unduly heated within itself, the unreason of man put for the reason of God. It would seem, therefore, that if we are to overpass the insight of the mind in any degree, the only and sufficient way of doing it, the way farthest removed from mysticism and those dark shadows of confusion and frailty which so easily rest on the human spirit, is this very way of verbal dictation. The mind may at last return to such a record later, with the hope of making something of it. Yet even then, if the truth is mastered, the truth and the spirit meet, in the instant of communication, on a level, and that level the level of naturalism. The feeling, therefore, which drives us away from verbal inspiration should carry us at once over to its only proper antithesis, the freedom of the human mind with the divine mind.

We thus escape the conflict of two distinct methods: the mind's self-contained search after truth, and the putting of truth upon it by an agency external to it. All forceful inspiration must be perplexed by this incongruity of processes. So far as the Scriptures are made up of familiar facts, so far as they are the record of personal feelings, the purely natural suffices, and must suffice, for their explanation. But between human products and the immediate products of the divine mind, there must be a marked cleavage. To find this cleavage, define it, and respect it, will be a point of first importance, and of hopeless perplexity, in exegesis.

Hence the doctrine of an authoritative inspiration has always been found more or less incompatible with free inquiry and thorough criticism. Christian men have had occasion, over and over again, to soften their notion of inspiration, and of the range of the truths dependent on it, in order to meet the new facts brought before them, and the growing temper of inquiry. The progress of truth has been delayed, and bitter and misleading discussions have arisen, because of the doctrine of inspiration. The facts of science, as in reference to the creation, have first been contemptuously rejected, then slowly received, and, last of all, made fully compatible with a modified view of the authority of the Scriptures. Free inquiry cannot readily proceed, when its path may be crossed at any moment by this line of cleavage which separates human thoughts and divine truths, the partial and the relative from the complete and the absolute. The doctrine of inspiration has not, empirically, justified itself as a means of entering into all knowledge. It gives occasion to the very strange assertion that complex spiritual truth, as it lies in the human mind, can be absolute. We thus reach a result the exact opposite of that we had in view. The doctrine of inspiration arises largely from diffidence, a distrust of human wisdom. We are compelled, however, in defence of the doctrine, to affirm that the most wide-reaching truths are complete and final in human knowledge. It thus cuts us off from that ever renewed inquiry into them which is at once the real modesty and true power of human thought.

The moral discipline of the world is thereby fundamentally disturbed. That discipline consists quite as much in finding the truth, in correcting and enlarging it, as in obeying it. Indeed, these two things are inseparable from each other. At no point ought this discipline to be more ample and obligatory than in connection with religious truth. But so far as inspiration renders this truth complete and final, it limits inquiry and arrests moral training. Religious truth is thrown out of harmony with other forms of truth, and religious action with the action of the world. Everywhere else investigation is in order, and is allowed freely to correct all previous conclusions. Not thus is it in faith, and the inevitable result follows. Human thought, in its freedom, lashes against these boundaries of the religious world, and the air is filled with needless confusion and clamor.

No strong tendency, however, is found in the spiritual world without some underlying reason. What is the reason which has so long sustained this doctrine of inspiration, and made it the very citadel of theological belief? It is, I think, our just sense of dependence on God, and our desire to be assured of his guidance. This feeling has given this belief, as it so readily does other truths, too exterior and mechanical a form. The great gifts of God are in ourselves. His chief aid is in the very action of our own powers. Everything else is quite secondary to this. The Kingdom of Heaven is within us. Inspiration properly means a breath of life, a living transfer of the divine thought to us, a free participation on our part in it. We deny a formal inspiration only that we may insist on a real one. We brush aside an external, ineffectual gift, only that we may accept an all-sufficing one in the mind itself. God does most for us, when we are doing most for ourselves; and we no longer make any division between the human and the divine in truth. It is all human, all divine; the atmosphere in which the spirit of man and the spirit of God meet each other. The spiritual displaces the mechanical, and when we think of God justly, God is present with us. His spirit is the spirit of truth, and testified within the mind itself. Truth is a living presence passing forever between mind and mind. Inspiration is always one thing, intelligence rejoicing in the light which floods the universe from the Divine Presence. We are not denying the doctrine, we are placing it on a more adequate and comprehensive foundation. We are identifying the method of God in Revelation with his universal method in the world. We are giving the actions of God the harmony and extension which belong to them. We are enforcing naturalism.

This belief of a sufficient and final statement of religious truth in the Scriptures lacks proof. Wanting clearness and inner coherence, it requires a degree and form of proof which it is difficult to furnish. If the Scriptures, by complete harmony and absolute correctness, so far as we can test these qualities, seemed to justify this claim of divine authorship; if the notion of divine authorship could be so framed as to include no incongruous terms; if the Scriptures themselves explicitly affirmed their supernatural origin, there might be an internal force in these concurrent facts that would carry conviction. But none of these things are present. There is much in the Scriptures which embarrasses this claim of infallible inspiration, and renders it hard to accept; the notion is not coherent within itself or analogous to the divine method in other directions; and the statements of the Bible on the subject are such as readily to receive a much less rigid interpretation.

If we were to look for external proof of this doctrine of divine intervention, and demand this evidence in a sufficient form, the unsustained assertions of the writers themselves would go but a little way in establishing the dogma. No man can testify to his own inspiration, or to the inspiration of another, in a conclusive form. The facts are too obscure, and admit of too easy misapprehension. This testimony must be sustained, as Christ said of his own testimony, by the witness of God. We should thus be compelled, under external proof, to call for a perfectly explicit assertion of superhuman intervention, and the direct support of the declaration by miraculous power. Moreover, the entire proof so made out, should be transmitted to us in a method beyond reasonable criticism. Any weakness in any of these particulars would so reduce the evidence as to destroy its irrefragable character. It belongs to so definite and so extraordinary a claim as this of divine aid, and one involving such ample resources, to be equally definite and startling in its vindication. The supernatural, when offered as a fact, must establish itself undeniably out of its own abundant means. A distinct, divine element in Revelation must not be so hidden and smothered by natural causes as to lose its true position. This is to breed hopeless confusion, and leave the mind without any secure footing.

The proofs actually offered of a transcendent inspiration are very far from meeting these claims. They are chiefly assertions in the New Testament made concerning the Old Testament, and one and all they easily accept the less rigid construction. Thus Paul says: " All Scripture is given by inspiration of God, and is profitable for reproof, for correction, for instruction in righteousness."[1] Certainly; this assertion is every way as true on the supposition that the mind of the writer, enveloped in the thought of God, is thoroughly possessed by the truth, as on the supposition that this truth is in any way pushed beyond his powers. Errors of thought and of expression do not prevent the profitableness of Scripture for reproof, correction, instruction. They rather put it on the same plane with our other terms of discipline in these purposes.

[1] 2 Tim. iii., 16.

Inspiration, in this passage, may as readily mean a normal, as an abnormal, action of mind.

Peter seems more explicit when he declares: "Prophecy came not in old time by the will of man, but holy men of God spake as they were moved by the Holy Ghost."[1] While we can put into these words the stronger form of inspiration, if our minds are already convinced, they readily receive the weaker one. The will of man is contrasted with holy men of God, and means not human action, but human action as separating itself from divine counsel. The antithesis lies between the obedient and the disobedient temper, and not between human thought and divine thought. The force we give to the words, "moved by the Holy Ghost," will turn on our apprehension of the office of the Holy Spirit, the Spirit of Truth. The coming of the Holy Spirit is especially emphasized by Christ. In his last address to his disciples he says: "I will pray the Father, and he shall give you another Comforter, that he may abide with you forever, the Spirit of Truth; whom the world cannot receive, because it seeth him not, neither knoweth him, but ye know him, for he dwelleth with you and shall be in you."[2] These assertions are not to be urged as promises of a special inspiration to accompany the disciples. This rendering is much too narrow. They are addressed through the disciples to us all. They stand for the general and comprehensive fact of the fellowship of all good men in spiritual truth with God, the eternal Spirit of Truth. Such a declaration as this, we live and move and have our being in God, should sweep from our thoughts, as by a whirlwind running before the Divine Presence, any notion of any particular and narrow and sub-conscious way in which a few favored minds are acted

---

[1] 2 Pet. i., 21.   [2] John xiv., 16, 17.

on of God. No; it would be the infinite misfortune of these elect disciples—shall I say of seclusion and mystery—not to have been fully brought forth into the light of the Spirit of Truth; not to have stood with the Word of God and the household of God in the open presence of God. The condition of a simple believer, living and moving and having his being in God, is one infinitely preferable to that of a disciple, so pressed upon and unfairly dealt with by the divine strength as to become the mouthpiece of truth beyond his own mastery. Such a separation of the inspired writer is to his own detriment and dishonor. God's methods are large, generous, general. They belong to all believers. He does for each of them the best possible thing. There is no hierarchy based on exceptional power or position. We all drink of the cup of Christ, and are baptized with his baptism.

"There is a spirit in man," says Job, "and the inspiration of the Almighty giveth them understanding."[1] What could it do less than this; what could it do more than this! Understanding is the inspiration of the Almighty. It is his own life. The entrance of the word giveth light. Thus Peter feels that he has right to the general exhortation: "If any man speak, let him speak as the oracles of God."[2] Yes, indeed, if any man speak, let him speak as the oracles of God.

The idea of inspiration is somewhat definitely disclosed by the sacred writers. So grand a thing is knowledge felt to be by them that, even in its inferior forms, and wrongful forms, it is referred to divine wisdom, and likened unto it. God is represented as saying concerning Bezaleel, the son of Uri, the son of Hur, of the tribe of Judah: "I have filled him with the spirit of God, in wisdom, and in

---

[1] Job xxxii., 8. [2] 1 Pet. iv. 11.

understanding, and in knowledge, and in all manner of workmanship to devise cunning works, to work in gold and in silver and in brass."[1] Not a more explicit statement is anywhere made of inspiration than is covered by the skill ascribed to this workman in gold and silver and brass. A little farther on it is said : " In the hearts of all that are wise-hearted I have put wisdom." It is also affirmed : " The counsel of Ahithophel, which he counselled in those days, was as if a man had inquired of the oracles of God."[2]

The Scriptures give us other indications of the nature of inspiration. Says Luke, in opening his gospel: " It seemed good to me also, having had perfect understanding of all things from the very first, to write unto thee in order, most excellent Theophilus, that thou mightest know the certainty of those things wherein thou hast been instructed." He does not so much as intimate that his words are to have any other authority than this of his personal knowledge ; a grievous mistake, certainly, if the real subscription of his gospel, giving it weight, is the divine autograph. In the presence of such a confirmation, other grounds of trust would be insignificant. The apostles claim authority for this testimony as eye-witnesses of the event. Is this then their authority, or is it not ?

The Gospels, like other portions of Scripture, taken in their relation to each other, declare, as conclusively as any set of facts can declare, their own character, that they were put together out of changeable and incomplete material, material so incomplete as to preclude either a consecutive or a full narrative. What is their weakness, from one point of view, goes far to establish their essen-

---

[1] Ex. xxxi., 3.   [2] 2 Sam. xvi., 23.

tial correctness. Their variety of form, taken in connection with their general coherence in spirit and substance, calls for that substratum of facts on which they claim to rest. We are thus indebted to the particular knowledge of Luke for the preservation of the two parables of the prodigal son and the good Samaritan, containing the most explicit development of the two factors of faith,—the love of God and the love of man—and to St. John for the full spiritual force of the words of Christ.

A sound mind cannot easily see the extent to which these thoroughly natural causes have been wrought into the very substance of the Gospels, determining what has been saved and what lost in the teachings and life of Christ, without feeling that this naturalism, which has been allowed such range among these most precious things, must be supreme throughout; that the words and acts of Christ, like all instruction from the beginning until now, were committed unreservedly to the flow of events. The seed was scattered, and fell, some by the wayside, some on good ground. Any other conclusion is incongruous, improbable, and so irrational. The force of circumstances declares itself everywhere. There is no divine intervention, correcting the confusion of the narrative, or supplying its deficiencies. We seem to be compelled to admit that the partial and confused knowledge that lies on the face of the Gospels expresses the real facts in the case.

If we contrast the Gospels with each other, we find discrepancies very unexpected on the supposition of an overruling inspiration, but perfectly natural, not to say unavoidable, if each author is left to make the best he can of his own resources. Even the Lord's Prayer is not given in the same words by the two evangelists, and one or both of the forms are, therefore, inaccurate. If these most select possible words are inexact, what is there that may not be so? If we compare the Sermon on the Mount as recorded by Matthew and by Luke, the agreement between the two renderings is sufficient to show that the writers have in view the same discourse, while the omissions and variations on the part of Luke indicate plainly that his knowledge, in this particular, was much less complete than that of Matthew. Indeed, his version of the beatitudes is so imperfect as to be liable, taken by itself, to mislead us as to their very spirit. Matthew says: " Blessed are the poor in spirit, for theirs is the kingdom of heaven." Says Luke: " Blessed be ye poor, for yours is the kingdom of God." Matthew tenderly affirms, " Blessed are they that mourn, for they shall be comforted"; Luke, in a temper much less subdued, declares, " Blessed are ye that weep now, for ye shall laugh." We can hardly doubt which is the more correct statement of the gentle, discriminating words of our Lord. A feeling of alarm passes over us at the danger we have incurred of missing the spiritual aroma that attended on the real utterances of Christ, by the imperfect version of some one evangelist.

It is hardly admissible, in the presence of such facts, to say that Matthew and Luke are alike preserved by divine intervention from material error. They are too plainly not kept from decided deficiency and partial mistakes. We may well think lightly of these discrepancies, if all we wish for is an open path to the mind of Christ; but if we are in search of explicit and final authority, this desire at once makes them serious. If we still insist that the evangelists are preserved from any serious error, we are putting ourselves on ground that is tenable only because it is vague and indefinite. No facts are a sufficient refutation of an erratic spirit of interpretation. As men of sound minds, we ought to meet all these weak defences of the highest truths with an earnest protest in the name of sober reason and simple righteousness. How exact and ample is the assertion of Peter: "Ye have purified your spirits in obeying the truth through the Spirit."[1] What other living office is there for the Spirit than that given by John: "He will guide you into all truth."[2] These processes of thought and action are perfectly normal, and we are not incautiously to allow any confusion to creep into them. If our theory is unsound, what will our results be under it? If we set aside reason in initiating inquiry, how shall we restore it in its progress?

Paul is especially relied on for dogmatic authority. But Paul's epistles, as the Epistle to the Romans, or the Epistle to the Galatians, are full of debate, argument, proof. What is the significancy of this fact? Evidently this: he is relying on the inner coherence, justness, and energy of his presentation for its authority. His force is that of discussion, and being that of discussion it is neither more nor less than it. Having finished the argument, he is not at liberty to say: These logical relations are not the grounds of my assertion, its real grounds are the informing words of the Holy Spirit. First to make an appeal to reason, and later to withdraw into the presence chamber of Deity, is illusive and dishonorable. If one should offer us conclusions which seemed to be wholly his own, and when he had called forth discussion and contradiction should proceed to quell it with the affirmation: These are simply the words of the highest authority on this subject, we should feel that we had been dealt with unfairly. We had been drawn into the field of debate by false appearances. Paul is not right in putting his own personality

[1] 1 Pet. i., 22.   [2] John xvi., 13.

back of his words to the degree in which he does, if, after all, it does not belong there; if he is tempting us to cross swords with him and then leaving us to shiver our weapons on the buckler of the Almighty. For my part I must have too exalted an opinion of St. Paul to believe that he ever did any such thing. If he was a divine herald of truth, one method, and one only, properly belonged to him, that of quiet, exact utterance of the message entrusted to him, as one resting on an authority infinitely beyond his own. Who is able to sort out things human and things divine when once commingled, and to assign each its true value?

His own view seems certainly to be, not this, sufficient and final authority, but this, an earnest search after truth. "We know in part and we prophesy in part." "Now we see through a glass darkly, but then face to face. Now I know in part, but then shall I know even as I am known."[1] This is his exhortation: "Having these gifts, differing according to the grace that is given us, whether prophecy, let us prophesy according to the proportion of faith."[2] With a noble humility and a divine courage, he says: "Brethren, I count not myself to have apprehended; but this one thing I do, forgetting the things which are behind and reaching forth unto the things which are before, I press forward toward the mark of the prize of the high calling of God in Christ Jesus."[3] Grand Apostle of Truth; let nothing intervene between our souls and thy soul, as nothing intervenes between thy soul and God. It is this fellowship of life with life, in one eternal movement toward God, that is alone regenerative in human experience. Is there not in these words of Paul something very like a direct testimony against a full

[1] 1 Cor. xiii., 9, 12.   [2] Rom. xii., 6.   [3] Phil. iii., 13.

and sufficient revelation of truth? This doctrine of inspiration carries with it immeasurable confusion when we are dealing with the expression of personal feeling, the poetic insight of David, the pathetic lament of Jeremiah, the forecast of Isaiah, the tenderness of John, the up-lift of St. Paul. These things must be human, genuine, through and through, or they sink into spiritual rubbish.

We cannot manage the personal element, which appears so frequently, so freely, and so profitably in Scripture, otherwise than by accepting it as perfectly sincere. Paul's estimate of faith, hope, and charity, contained in the thirteenth chapter of the first Epistle to the Corinthians, must be understood as the product of his own experience; and his fervid exclamation in the eighth of Romans, opening with the words, "Who shall separate us from the love of Christ," must be rejoiced in as the fulness of his own affection.

One is also justified in supposing that if the apostles were under a complete protection against error in spiritual things, this fact would have shown itself in their words and actions as well as in their writings; in their handling of the early churches under the circumstances of peculiar perplexity and danger which they encountered. We must have the strongest reasons for asserting an inspiration in their written words which we do not find in their spoken words. When the Gospel began to be freely preached to the Gentiles, and accepted by them, the relation of these converts to the Jewish church and to Jewish observances came before an apostolic synod at Jerusalem for settlement. While a wise and acceptable conclusion was reached, it is quite certain that a good deal of diversity of opinion and feeling appeared among the apostles, and that this division of sentiment remained a long time. St. Paul and St. James occupied extreme positions, while St. Peter vacillated somewhat between them. Paul's account of the synod, given in the second chapter of Galatians, shows that the irritation of the discussion was considerable, lingered many years in the differences it involved, and frequently embarrassed him in his work. "Those who seemed to be somewhat, whatsoever they were, it maketh no matter to me: God accepteth no man's person; for they who seemed to be somewhat"—James, Peter, and John—"in conference added nothing to me."

This difference of view is so far reproduced in the epistles of Paul and of James, that acute and earnest exegetes have been unable to reconcile the two statements. A fact of such supreme importance, in the early history of the Church, as this of the divided feeling of the apostles on the manner of extending the Gospel does not accord with the supposition of a divine guidance that precluded error of doctrine. The apostles seem to have been left, like the servants of truth everywhere, to make what shift they could in reaching their conclusions and doing their work. No exception was made in their behalf to the universal method. But if they were not able to guide themselves perfectly under the most critical and important circumstances, how shall they guide us without error? Though much more importance has been attached to these differences of opinion than belongs to them, they evidently involved some error and limitation of view.

We have now said enough to show that we have no burden of proof to overcome in rejecting a doctrine of inspiration that carries the impulse toward truth off the plane of human powers. We are at full liberty, therefore, to consider the historic results of this doctrine, and the mischievous part it has played in theology. Dogmatic development tends to three phases. The truth which lies back of any dogma is first held freely, uncritically, with changeable definition. The truth is submissive to a living purpose in the feelings and actions. The period of analysis has not come. The thoughts have not yet turned back on themselves in the process of exposition and defence. Later, under the push of speculation and unbelief, doctrine is turned into definite dogma, which the believer is called on to accept under specific terms. The chief interest of this phase of movement is intellectual, not vital. Still later, when these limits of thought are found to be insufferable bounds, robbing the truth and the mind under the truth of their proper liberty, they are broken over, and belief is taken up again into a more spiritual experience, with deeper and more personal insight, and with more living service. What the truth thus loses in precision, it far more than gains in scope and power. Henceforth it ranks with those divine things which give light without themselves being fully disclosed in the light. In this process of development, partial and misleading images are cast aside; rigid terms of definition are burned up in the heat of the mind's action; and the conceptions under consideration come to be held, like moisture in the atmosphere, as life-giving terms, capable of many, most variable, most beautiful manifestations, no one of them final. The dogmatic period is transitional between a lower and higher use of truth. It lies between conceptions less purified and spiritualized, and those more purified and spiritualized. It is a hasty crystallization of the truth, but it aids in separating its real substance from an obscure admixture of sensuous elements. The dogma is dissolved again in a purer medium the moment the growing mind calls for it in its living processes; and in each of these dissolutions and distillations and crystallizations, it gains additional purity. This movement of thought is every way wholesome. The storm-clouds that lie low and massive and threatening, when the winds have passed and the tumult ceased, reappear serene, orderly, infinitely peaceful in the upper air.

The engine, with sharp puff and visible power, flings out in the frosty air great billowy masses of vapor and smoke, full of expansive force. This voluminous and luminous mass is pervaded by the inherent energies which create it. As the engine passes on, this streamer of clouds is slowly dissolved. The vapor, its potent term, is absorbed in the atmosphere, and the smoke, its dead term, remains a dark trail behind it. So in a dogmatic controversy, instinct with living tendencies, the power of spiritual convictions is quickly reabsorbed, while the verbal deposit lingers only to obscure and cloud the horizon, and mark the path that has been left behind.

The doctrine of the Trinity assumed form in the midst of theosophic and Gnostic speculations. Occult conceptions, foreign to our experience and alien to the Christian temper, find expression in it. In the eternal begetting of the Son, and the perpetual procession of the Spirit from the Son and the Father, we are in the midst of images which have no explanatory power. The doctrine of the atonement received its most explicit statement at a time when Roman law was in full revival, and common law was beginning to move in its fountains. The result was a narrow, governmental view of our relations to God, which we have been slowly casting off ever since. The smoke of the cloud could not be absorbed in the spiritual atmosphere as a medium of life, and we have waited long for it to fall to the earth as cinder and dust.

The doctrine of inspiration reached its rigid and exact statement in the scholastic period of reformed theology; the period which followed its first years of protest and strength. Protestant theologians, having broken with the church and with tradition, sought authority, in a period in which authority was chiefly external and counted for much, in the Scriptures. They pushed the doctrine to the full extent of verbal inspiration. This conclusion was the opaque element obstructive to vision, and we are still waiting for a pure and pellucid medium between us and the works of God, between us and God. The slow separation has gone on, however, and there now remains to many Christian minds only one trace of darkness, the arbitrary assertion that the Spirit is present in Scripture for the positive anticipation of error in spiritual things. This is the last, low trail of the cloud that covered half the heavens.

The uses of the doctrine of inspiration—by no means unimportant, times, places, and persons being considered—have shown two forms of unequal value, and often of conflicting force. This doctrine aims at authority, and finds for it a pivotal point in the Scriptures. It was the desire for authority, and the supposed need of authority, which carried the doctrine in expression from point to point, till a final defence was set up in the assertion of the absolute verbal completeness of the divine message.

This desire for authority in religious faith involves different and diverse tendencies. It may come in satisfaction of an intellectual and spiritual craving for assured truth in a region of peculiar doubts and difficulties. The soul covets rest and casts itself freely on a belief that promises support. The sense of personal feebleness and confusion is met by the doctrine. But a very different and much less commendable feeling is often involved in this desire for authority. It is not rest for our own spirits that is sought for so much as conclusions that we can lay peremptorily upon others. The strength of the Church is felt to be the infallibility of its faith, and each zealous disciple becomes much in earnest to affirm and to share this infallibility. The doctrine then arises in satisfaction of the wish to rule, so universally present to men. Those who hold the doctrine for this end easily fall into the condemnation of Christ: " For ye have taken away the key of knowledge; ye entered not in yourselves, and them that were entering in ye hindered." [1]

This desire for authority, this desire to arrest inquiry, as having fulfilled its purpose, is, in the world of personal, spiritual experiences, a mistake. It means a point of support taken outside the mind itself, not the poise and rest of the mind within itself. Authority arises in suspension of the inner life of the soul. Its *dicta* become an indigestible something, incapable of assimilation, which has found its way into the food of the spirit. At no point does the divine method differ more broadly and fundamentally from the human method than at this point of authority. The very gist of divine nurture is to hold us steadily to the double duty of discovering and obeying the truth. We cannot well obey truth, till we can also understand it. The two processes demand the same temper, and something of the same wisdom. Formal obedience, divorced from diligent inquiry, easily loses the very nature of virtue. A mistake in the method of faith may readily become a mistake in the very substance

[1] Luke xi., 52

of faith, and quite mislead the mind. The bat, hanging head downward by hooks on his wings, is not more unlike the bird, riding restfully on the brisk wind, than is the mind, subjected to authority, unlike the mind that seeks freely unto God. To accept authority in religious truth is to run the risk of falling into the hands of religious rulers, and being employed for the most mischievous purposes of tyranny.

This subject of authority is obscure with us, because we mingle, in its discussion, very different things. We confuse the spiritual ordering of the thoughts with the outward control of the actions by religious organizations. Men, in all stages of development, seek earnestly for authority in society, which stands with them for peace, strength, and good order. The Church, as clothed with power, has been a primary means of construction. This beneficent service we associate with its authoritative interpretation of truth. But the limits of ecclesiasticism, as a form of government, are being reached. Those who think otherwise may still find spiritual control, in its most effective form, in the Catholic Church. It is the true mission of Protestantism to appeal to the liberty of the mind with the truth, and this appeal can accept no new limitations. It arises the moment thought is vigorous enough to claim its own laws of development, and assert itself as sufficient unto itself within its own spiritual realm.

The masses of men may still need instruction in their search into religious truth, and personal influence in their obedience to it. This fact modifies, without altering, the fitness of freedom. Protestantism cannot vacillate between the old and the new. It must accept its own principles, and live by them. It strives in vain to maintain the shreds of ecclesiastical authority by attaching an extraneous force to the truth, aside from its appeal to the mind. The order it strives to induce in society is a purely spiritual one, and, in attaining this order, it must fully accept the conditions it has laid down for itself.

The doctrine of inspiration has deepened dissent and division in Protestant churches. It has enforced the letter, as opposed to the spirit, and made the devotees of faith blind and refractory from the outset. When a believer has laid hold of an exact statement,—as Luther of the words, This is my body,—it has been found impossible to shake him loose. Every verbal difference has been a barrier to be fought over with inexhaustible bitterness. If a free appeal to reason had been open, much confusion would have readily disappeared. But such an appeal was precluded by the doctrine of inspiration, and by the dogmatic temper attendant on it. The letter was not freely dissolved in the spirit, and so ready to crystallize again in obedience to the inner, rational movement. The soul became blind and bigoted by a false adhesion to misapplied symbols. A judicial temper was lost, and a confused and obstinate one took its place. What inexhaustible stores of fanaticism and folly have been found in The Revelation. This one book, by its abuse, has blighted many a spirit which it should have blessed.

When one begins to talk about the number of the beast, and make up the sum of years which lies between us and the millennium, we feel that he is hopelessly dropping off from the Divine Mind as disclosed in the march of events.

The effort to secure authority has resulted in the loss

of authority, a device to prevent division has increased division, and discussion of peculiar bitterness has grown out of that which forbade discussion. The army of believers has been scattered and peeled, wrangling over innumerable trifles, and unable to see the sun in the heavens. The sharp, acrimonious strife over the bread and the wine, over the form of baptism, over the seventh day and Sunday, offers such a tithing of mint, anise, and cumin, as was scarcely surpassed in the Jewish Church. Mind and heart have been alike blinded and blasted by this turning of small things into large ones. God's world has been hidden behind one's fingers.

The search for authority, we have seen, is double, authority in support of trembling faith, and authority against recalcitrant faith. Not only did external authority put irreconcilable division between believers, it ultimately weakened faith within the soul itself. This has been the second grave mistake in the doctrine of inspiration, a mistake that stands in bold relief theoretically and historically—the loss of the hold of the mind on truth as truth. The doctrine has acted in contradiction of the words of Christ: Ye shall know the truth, and the truth shall make you free. If there is one fundamental thing which the Christian Church has lacked, in a conspicuous way; one fundamental thing which it should have possessed in a conspicuous degree, it has been tolerance, an earnest and wide search for truth, and a patient holding fast to it in tenderness.

The spirit of science has risen in the assembly of the saints to administer well-deserved censure. The failure of the Church to nourish a truth-loving, truth-seeking temper is attributable, in large part, to this very doctrine of inspiration. The Church was supposed to possess perfect truth, and had, therefore, no occasion to go in search of it. Those who ventured out of beaten paths were thought of not as eager inquirers in the world of Revelation, but as foolish adventurers, wickedly forsaking the old ways. That which made this independent search more difficult, made it also, when undertaken, more dangerous. The mind was thrown, to begin with, into a defiant, rash attitude, and found itself at every step unsustained and uncorrected. A headlong, resentful temper bore it on toward error. Nothing can well be more oppugnant to an indwelling of the spirit of truth in the minds of all, than this bondage to the letter, which attends on any complex statement as a final form of thought. No matter how simple the words may be, religious principles are immeasurable in their scope. The divine impulse may at any moment transcend its previous terms.

This conception of inspiration is inapplicable to higher forms of truth. Truth is not a verbal proposition. It is the inner, visible coincidence of thought and the subject of thought. As long as we are dealing with words, we are missing ideas, we are missing truth. No matter how correct any given formula may be, when offered to us, it holds no truth till we too see its relation to the facts covered by it. Truth is the insight of the mind, nothing less, nothing more. A divine push, that pushes the mind off this balance of thought, is violence in the spiritual world. Words are paper currency in the exchange of thought, and owe their value to their power to command the coin of truth. Used otherwise, they are illusive symbols of value, and not value itself. To give, therefore, authority to words, or to an irreconcilable conception that lies back of them, is the worst possible sin against the truth, since it blocks all farther pursuit of it, all possible approach to it.

This seems very plain, when we are dealing with the more profound forms of truth. Who would think of understanding mathematics otherwise than by understanding it, or penetrating the divine purpose in the government of the world otherwise than by penetrating it! There are some limited and comparatively barren statements of facts which can be made to us in words, rendered by us in familiar images, and accepted without any insight. But these assertions lie in a narrow, sensuous experience, and play a very small part in Revelation. Revelation, as a profound fact, is understanding the mind of God, and this means that our thoughts are keeping pace with his thought, that our spiritual experiences are touching their meridian in the noontide of his presence.

Strangely enough, when the Apostle Peter states twice over, quite explicitly, a simple fact that transcends our knowledge, and yet comes within the forms of imagination, the preaching of Christ to the spirits in prison, a large share of the Christian Church turns from the assertion as one inconsistent with previous convictions. If revelation of unknown events—a direction in which revelation is most possible—is sought for, here it is, and yet it is here to very little purpose. It is well for us to remember that from this most obvious form of a supernatural disclosure the Scriptures keep quite aloof.

The one divine attitude, on our part, is teachableness, a meekness and poverty of spirit which are slowly enriched by the kingdom of Heaven. We must not account ourselves to have attained, but, forgetting the things that are behind, press forward toward the mark of the prize of our high calling in Christ Jesus. Certainly, timid and feeble minds can be helped, but they must be helped on the basis of naturalism and not off of it. Otherwise they sink into hopeless dependence, spiritual pauperism, and are peculiarly liable, under any sudden trial, to drop into unbelief.

The slovenly reasoning we often meet with in the religious world, the narrow outlook from a single window thrown open for a specific purpose, should pass away, and we should learn to meet God in his own world, in his own large way, through the entire range of his providences. We should follow Christ heedfully as he moves among men, letting fall his blessings on those who are nearest to him. If fundamental truth is ever and always that which discloses to us the mind of God, then inspiration, in its higher forms, must be insight, understanding Christ, when we are with him, behold his works, and hear his words.

The apparent reverence expressed by the doctrine of inspiration is often deceitful, and simply puts the mind in bondage to human authority. The echo and re-echo of dogma in the region of dialectics take from us the simplicity and purity of heart by which we see God. We have no inner habit by which we find our way alone into the Divine Presence. Among the various renderings of the Scripture, we accept that as inspired with which we are familiar. We are bowing to a divine authority, but it is an authority which is expressed to us in a very human way, by very fallible men. The entire relation of man to God is embarrassed. Instead of inquiring directly into the truth, we are put upon an indirection in which men and systems and interpretations and transmissions play a leading part. The soul, seeking unto God, is fairly caught in the net of churchcraft. If thine eye is single, it shall be full of light. The importance attached to some deviation from an established standard greatly increases this confusion, and leaves the mind worn out, and its strength wasted, by the mere accidents of sound thought.

A faulty form of inspiration mingles hopelessly the natural and the supernatural. We meet with no difficulty in the supernatural; we accept it with lightness and gladness of heart; we believe it to stand in living relations with the natural, and so standing, to be the sensible joy of the Divine Presence. As the higher powers of man are first rooted in his physical endowments, and, deeper down, in the very soil of the earth, and yet preserve their transcendent character, so the supernatural, in its true form, is the very flower and fragrance of the natural, the vanishing point of physical laws as they are taken up into the divine purpose—clouds that are losing form and color and melting into the blaze of light about them.

We cannot understand the world without the living, spiritual presence of God in it, and the miraculous is this presence in its most sensuous form; the mind and heart, of God overpassing, with a little intensity of emphasis, their ordinary expression. A supernatural, therefore, which arises in fulfilment of the natural, is in most profound sympathy with it, is the voice of the speaker, in fitting intonation, ringing the thought on its way; is the light and heat with which the electric current discloses its presence. The supernatural is deeply affiliated with the inmost force of faith, and rational life.

We take objection to the Divine Presence which attends on the doctrine of inspiration, not because it is supernatural, but because it enters in suspension of the highest form of the natural, the insight of mind; because it substitutes for the purest impulse of reason in the human soul, we know not what obscure and blind tendency; because it represents God as acting, not as we find him acting, a God of order, but as one of confusion. This method gives us heat, without light; is not so much a tongue of flame resting harmlessly on men, as one of fire burning them up. A repression of human power has always gone with this controlling sense of the divine hand. The thoughts of men, the activities of men, have been overborne by it, and the spirit of truth has been sought rather as a power to quicken the dead than as one to give more life to the living, more wisdom to counsel, more coherence to labor, more justification to hope. There has thus arisen a deep-seated tendency to displace the earthly life with the heavenly life, rather than to make the one the harmonious prelude of the other; to invoke with importunate and painful prayer a divine intervention, rather than to fill full, sweetly full, with pure waters, all the fountains and streams of our present being. The supernatural has overwhelmed the natural, and so has lost its own right to be, and to be believed in. This is a most fatal mistake, and has given rise to much of the unbelief that now attends on religion. If nature and faith are found in conflict, there can be no doubt with which the victory will rest.

Inspiration, real inspiration, is the light that springs up at the point of highest, most harmonious, union of the natural and the supernatural, the human and the divine, in their perpetual passage into each other in all wisdom and righteousness. The natural, by itself alone, is dead, the body without the soul, the word without the idea; the supernatural, breaking in on and displacing the natural, is a stress of life too great for the physical, intellectual powers which sustain it, a meaning so intense as to strangle the forms of speech through which it struggles to express itself. As long as God is the immanent soul of things, let us not fear to handle freely the divine thought, let us make sure rather that we are dealing with this thought, declared in the full light of day, and not with the phosphorescent gleams of decaying things, superstitions that still flicker on the horizon of belated spirits. Inspiration is the rational extension of the divine thought in the minds of men. Knowledge as knowledge involves the highest, most normal, activity of mind. This activity is nourished on two sides: by what we know as nature, in the narrow use of the word—strictly causal relations; and by what we know as the supernatural, a divine presence in these fixed relations, both ordering and extending them. Knowledge contains in itself both terms,—the fixed and the free, the thing comprehended and the comprehending power—and demands them both in all its higher acts of acquisition.

If we insist that a determinate inspiration pervades the Scriptures, or even their spiritual truths,—though it certainly is not easy to separate between the historic facts and the moral principles they contain—we put all the difficulties, and the growing difficulties, of exegesis at their maximum, and make any material failure to meet them fatal. We carry our costly vase in our hands, yet to drop it once is to shatter it utterly. The authority of the Bible, and so our view of its value, are imperilled at every step of interpretation, and we are tempted to shield it in many disingenuous ways. It has thus suffered wreck and rescue many times already. A single rock may be fatal to the bravest ship that ever floated, and one failure may destroy the whole fabric of faith, built up on this extravagant claim. A double evil follows: many persons are precipitated into entirely needless unbelief; and many, evading this result, become flimsy and insufficient in thought, unprogressive and narrow in action, and unspiritual in the very substance of their lives. The theological mind, instead of sharing to the full the extraordinary impulse of our times; instead of making the divine character tally with the enlarging revelation of it in the world, has often been busily occupied, in the last half century, in contending against the progress of knowledge, and with futile contrivances to protect its own theories. What should have been a heavenly discipline, infinitely enlarging faith, has been productive of miserable makeshifts, stupid denials, reluctant concessions, half apprehensions. Such an attitude confirms unbelief in the unbelieving, and divides the religious camp into hostile factions, chafing under the endless collisions of the progressive and the dogmatic temper.

The indescribable and bitter bigotry of the mediæval era, begetting all narrowness of thought and cruelty of method, resting like the shadow of a wrathful heavens on the whole community, issuing in an insane sacrifice of human life, instead of passing utterly away, has given place but slowly to a crabbed temper that makes each necessary concession too late to escape its evils, too incomplete to use its fruits in growth.

It is not easy to do the devout mind a more serious injury than this of putting the moral and the religious impulse in conflict. One or other of the two strongholds of our spiritual nature is weakened, our confidence in moral law or our confidence in its personal equivalent in the character of God. There is no more fundamental harmony in our personal development than that which should lie between ethical law and religious sentiment, between the government of the world and our conception of the mind of God. Yet the two are constantly falling apart, a fact often due to the irrefragable character given to dogma by this doctrine of inspiration. Religious men may come to entertain a kind of spite toward scientific inquiry and ethical truth, as if they were in some way enemies of religion. This they never can be save by a strange perversion of knowledge and morality on the one hand, or of religion on the other. The first and second great commands are not more closely united than are morality and religion, knowledge and the will of God.

This possible conflict between a moral precept and a command of God—as if the two were not necessarily the same—is brought out in the attempted sacrifice of Isaac by Abraham, and the ordinary interpretation of it. In this narrative and its exegesis the very human lesson of implicit, blind obedience is put forward, and the very divine lesson of patient, rational inquiry hidden behind it. Our ready acceptance of the story, in its literal form, grows out of the easy adhesion of our untrained thoughts to the miraculous, and the reluctance with which we take up the lessons of truth on their strictly natural basis. It is a strange perversion of the divine method to suppose that God, by a miraculous intervention, commanded Abraham to violate the plainest principles of morality, and then left him in the confusion of thought thus begotten as a trial of faith. Nothing could well be more opposed to our experience of the ways of God. Such devices would institute a hopeless conflict between the sober duties of life and our religious conceptions concerning them. If we suppose Abraham not yet wholly to have escaped from surrounding influences and the sense of the fitness of human sacrifice, and—as has been suggested—that this narrative marks the culmination of the struggle in his own life, then all is clear, and an inadmissible conception is no longer laid upon our credulous and overburdened faith.

Like perplexities are constantly brought to us in the

study of the Old Testament by the absolute character given to its teachings. Things fundamentally wrong are passed upon as essentially right, and we are not allowed to understand them, in the only way in which they can bring us any instruction, as the products of the time and place to which they belonged. The mind thus loses its proper outlook on truth, its own advanced position, the training of God for thousands of years.

If, on the other hand, we accept the Bible for what it so plainly is, a growing revelation, a slow finding by men of their way among spiritual things, the dangers and difficulties of interpretation disappear. The shell drops from the kernel, and no edible portion is wasted. The Bible loses nothing and gains much. Slight flaws in the head of an axe are of no moment, flaws in its cutting edge are fatal. The view that we urge leaves the cutting edge of truth entire, and transfers defects to the dead weight that drives it.

If we are confronted with the fact that God is represented as offended with David for numbering the children of Israel, and as inflicting a severe punishment on the entire nation for this fault of the ruler, we have only to reply, "Thus imperfectly did David conceive the divine character," and the criticism drops at once to the ground, like chaff from wheat. The imprecatory psalms do not hide the lustre of those of worship; nor the pessimism of Ecclesiastes—"vanity of vanities, all is vanity"—burden the faith of Isaiah, beating its way heavenward with unwearied wing. If St. Paul mistakenly expected the second coming of Christ, the fact offers no difficulty; it is only our false attitude toward his opinion that is troublesome to us. If truth is simply the inexhaustible light of divine love, it is immaterial exactly where that light falls, or how much of it seems to be lost. Like the light of day in unclean or in desolate places, it is always pure and forever unmeasured; thus is it with a divine message in the mouths of men. What subversion of first truths, what horrible fanaticism, what far-reaching cruelty have been accelerated by the story of the witch of Endor and the command, "Thou shalt not suffer a witch to live." Sound thought has given way before this injunction, and thousands of lives have been sacrificed to it; and that, too, in a matter which touches most intimately the government of God.

We sum up the difficulties we find in complete inspiration with the comprehensive objection, that it prevents that constant reconstruction of religious truth which properly belongs to all times, and for which our own time is peculiarly ripe. If there is any one principle obvious in itself, and thoroughly enclosed in the laws of mind, a principle completely incorporated in the world about us, a principle that embraces all spiritual exhortation and scriptural motive, it is this very principle of religious progress, an unfolding of the minds and hearts of men toward God, a mastery in society of all divine impulses, a spreading abroad of the light and life of God till his kingdom is fully with us. But an inspiration that claims to give us anything like a perfect statement of truth, as contrasted with an inspiration that simply puts the mind, under its special powers and phases of development, in living contact with the truth, checks spiritual unfolding, and often holds us back from the divine ministration nearest to us. If the truths of the Bible, or any portion of its complex principles, are complete, if nothing can be added to them and nothing taken from them, then these truths must be known to us in this perfection, and no longer remain to be inquired into. A verbal statement that is absolute, but not understood, is a deceptive idea. Language owes its power to the meaning it imparts. Language that conveys no idea has no significance, and language that imperfectly conveys its idea is, to that degree, imperfect. If the doctrine of complete inspiration is to avail anything, we must accompany it with the assertion of our own power perfectly to measure the truth given us in the Scriptures, and, as its leading principles are there dealt with, to catch the breadth and fathom the depth of the divine mind. But if we contrast this bold statement with our feeble and contradictory attainments in knowledge, with the real insight of any body of theologians, it seems both foolish and profane. We have not yet seen that body of men who, collectively or singly, have had any right to plant themselves across the path of the divine word among men. It required a vision three times repeated to get the Apostle Peter out of the way of truth in a single, simple particular.

We do not escape this dilemma by saying that the Scriptures are complete, but not completely understood. A perfection of this sort can subserve no purpose of authority. It is a perfection, by the very supposition, unverifiable, since it is not yet reached. The Bible is to us what we understand it to be, and no more. We are liable, by this sophistical form of thought, to commit again that deep offence against reason—holding fast an untenable dogma by a trick of words. Truth must be left in theory in that incomplete form in which we find it in practice, if we are to understand our duty under it, and our method of inquiry into it; if we are to be led by the providence of God and by his growing revelation heavenward. We are in danger of throwing away the present in favor of the past, of losing God's gifts to us by our veneration of his gifts to others, of building the tombs of the prophets and slaying the prophets themselves.

The time has come in which the spiritual mind should turn from dogmas to facts—dogmas that have arisen from a speculative expansion of single, partial, and inadequate ideas, till, from a cloud the size of a man's hand, they have come to brood in darkness over the whole heavens; facts in the physical and spiritual world, that are springing this very day with creative power from the mind of God, and, under the light of his revealing spirit, are laying open to us from a new and higher position the divine counsel. The time has come to turn from logical discussion to ethical law—discussion that has exhausted and frittered away in dissection the ideas it once contained; ethical law that is regnant in the world of thought and action as never before. This emigration from the old to the new,—an emigration that carries with it all the wealth of the past, an emigration that enters on the virgin fields that historic forces have prepared for us,—this emigration the growth of knowledge is forcing upon us, and in it the living energies of God are waiting to lead us. It is a fresh call as significant as that of Abraham. True science is natural theology, which runs before and behind, above and beneath, all theology; that receives, as a dispersing atmosphere, the solid beams of light that enter it from without, and converts them into a genial, universal disclosure of the things nearest to us. We have converted science, so far as we readily could, into an enemy by struggling with its conclusions, rejecting its corrections, and turning aside from its inspirations. If Christian thinkers had awakened with the day, and diligently sought all traces of God's presence, and of his moral government, in the world, we should now be able to meet physical law with spiritual law, the outer perfection of form with the inner force of idea; and God immanent in the world, the world, the immediate expression of Divine Being, would be convictions flowing in on us every moment, as the light of all our life. This is to be the issue, and we are delayed in attaining it because we will not let go the past, we will not accept the more perfect in place of the less perfect conception, we will not relax our hold on dogma—the hand already rigid in its desperate clutch—till it is wrenched from us; and then we sink, many of us, into unbelief, like spent swimmers.

There are two errors equally errors, though not equally false: the tendency to shape our lives by our beliefs, and the tendency to shape our beliefs by our lives. The first tendency is incipiently right, and shows its failure only later in its rigidity. The second is incipiently wrong, and, with a flickering of light here and there, walks into deeper and deeper darkness. While belief properly initiates life, it should be in constant action and reaction with it. Life should enlarge its truths, correct its errors, and lead it to higher and yet higher points of observation. A belief that runs in advance of life, and is not renewed by it, will either consume, with ascetic heat, many beautiful things, or maintain itself one side of real life, in dull denial of it. Thought and action must live by one process, in one household, if they are to live at all.

If, in place of a supernatural inspiration, we accept an inspiration which is the immediate revelation of truth to the minds of men, a revelation that is human, because it is measured by the thoughts of men, which is divine, because it flows from the one fountain of truth and leads us to it, we shall have quite another view of the nature of duty, quite another disclosure of the path of ascent toward God. So true is this, that very few are willing, even while asserting the absoluteness of religious truth, to affirm the complete sufficiency of their own dogmas. Yet what less than this can they say to any purpose. If we are to be clear and coherent in our thought we must not hold on to absolute truth and progressive truth as parts of the same system. The absolute admits of no new light, no change of position; the relative calls constantly for both. We must say of ourselves, in contrast with all men, we are right and they are wrong.

Inquiry, if it proceeds, must be allowed to bring new construction to the entire system of truth. On no other terms is it appropriate. Nothing can remain intact except by an isolation that cuts it off from the living fellowship of faith. Growth must modify all that comes within its range. If growth is applicable to religious truths, we must let it have its way among all religious conceptions. Duty ceases to be holding fast what we have, and consists, by means of it, in seeking what we have not yet attained. We are pressing forward toward the mark of the prize of our high calling in Christ Jesus. Our own discipline is sought by us, the world is of interest to us, the kingdom of heaven is ours, as all equally involving a movement forward under the truth and toward the truth. The use of truth in action, and the disclosure of truth in thought, become more and more one and the same expansive process, that allows no limits and accepts no delays. Duty is thus constantly the building of a new and larger kingdom within the mind and without it, an entering into fresh light, the rectification of conduct and character under it, and a reconstruction of personal, social, and civil relations in harmony with the enlarging spiritual world. Thought and action lie together at the living centre of growth, and this growth is not a process of private significance merely, but spreads abroad, far and wide, like the buds of a tree, in the warm, glowing atmosphere which belongs to the race of men, dealt with collectively by God. Duty thus becomes a new thing, a more divine thing. It is not keeping clean and consecrate a temple already built; it is not holding fast an order already established; it is helping to build a new temple out of material just coming to light; it is carrying forward insufficient terms of order toward that more perfect conception of which they are the rudiments; it is working with God and seeing God work with us, as cosmic terms take form under the divine purpose which they contain.

Equally does the notion of inspiration, as the living presence of God with us, reinterpret life for us. Life has thus an integrity it cannot otherwise attain. There is no dead material in it; certainly not in the higher ranges of truth. We understand, we feel, we obey, we live. We live, and in living we enlarge action, feeling, knowledge. The words of prophets and apostles are translucent terms in Revelation, giving color to the light, receiving color from it—genuine products of the movement to which they belong. We find in St. Paul deep convictions, glowing feelings, a spiritual nature profoundly moved by the truth, but we find in him no law laid upon us. We may share his life, because we share his liberty in it. Truth, as a mere abstraction, perishes in many minds, because it fails really to enter them. It must perish in all minds that do not turn it into a personal experience. What the cloud is to the sunlight, gathering it and glorifying it, that is the mind to the message of truth. It·is living experiences that are the real terms of revelation.

Christ himself becomes an incarnation; in his life and action God gives a disclosure of divine love. The spiritual distance between understanding a truth and the power to utter that truth is a finite one. He who can apprehend the words of apostles, could, standing in the current of historic revelation, have uttered them. Revelation is this bringing of truth within the sweep of human thought, and human thought within the sweep of the truth. The highest minds, like the highest mountains, catch the light first, and reflect it longest; but it is lost in inapproachable space till these summits are touched by it. Down their slopes it glides rapidly, resting upon the entire plain. It is a strange inversion of thought to suppose that what the apostles could not grasp, may yet become a revelation in the minds of their disciples; that light may be present below, which has not been first present above. The integrity of our own lives, the integrity of the lives of God's servants, must make the movement of the mind under the truth genuine, through and through, from inception to completion.

What wisdom of exegesis comes to us the moment we direct the attention simply to the facts. The Old Testament is apprehended only as it is interpreted historically. The principles it contains are to be judged as principles, and their growth through the ages gratefully recognized. This fact granted, we inquire at our leisure, and with perfect safety of thought, into the precise circumstances which attended on their utterance. The truth of principle, the one invaluable thing, is surely with us, and needs no confirmation beyond itself.

We often have hard work, in the confidence of hope, to hold fast immortality. Is it not because religion is with us, to such a degree, a supernatural revelation, and not, what it might be, a personal experience, native to the world about us? We hold it as a relatively alien thing on outside authority, and not as indigenous life sealed in our own spirits. So far as we are full of spiritual life, we shall have no doubt of immortality. Confidence, push, buoyant power, belong to life, and compel it to take possession of its own field. The spirit, instinct with life, will assert that life, and stretch upward toward immortality in its fulfilment. If life is weak, the sense of immortality must sink with it.

This belief in God, as ever and equally with us, gives us also a new view of his method of work. The kingdom of heaven is not delayed as a matter of divine counsel, it is pushed forward as rapidly as its own nature and the mastery it must win over the hearts of men will allow. There is a true evolution in the spiritual world, a passage from darkness into light, a birth of the higher and holier in the region of the lower and less pure, a slow shaping of all the conditions of life to life, till it is made dominant within and without. This movement is, from beginning to end, a living process, a self-conscious progress, an inner triumph of pure reason, pure love, and one which cannot, therefore, for an instant, in any part of it, be thrown off its own rational centre. Its haste is an inner fervor, its fervor a growing conviction, its conviction the unfolding of truth within the soul itself by its own experience. To this end God is pouring his own life into the hearts of men as rapidly as they can, or they will, receive it. The whole process is life fed by life, and this divine gestation cannot shorten its own periods. The light of reason waits on it, and would at once be turned into darkness and death by any violence done to it. Any touch of force is violence, and nothing is life but the liberty of the spirit. The length of time it takes us to understand this fact is only another enforcement of our lesson that progress is a thing of growth.

The historic flood is let in; the wheels of motion are all spinning under it. What has been done, what shall be done, are, one and all, a continuous creation, a growing dawn, a revelation that cannot stop, or retreat on itself, or be at strife with itself, or be pushed beyond itself. A pagan dispensation, a Jewish dispensation, a Christian dispensation, are stages in the free, yet irresistible, universal coming of the kingdom of heaven; the fruit of a movement they do not measure; stars that, ushering in the day, are swallowed up by it. We may say, in the rapt spirit of the apostles: "For all things are yours, whether Paul, or Apollos, or Cephas, or the world, or life, or death, or things present, or things to come; all are yours; and ye are Christ's; and Christ is God's."

We have thus a more just sense of the momentum and majesty of the divine movement. It spreads over the whole earth and through all years; it gathers together in one all things, whether in heaven or on earth. It is not a flash of light, a sudden flush in the sky, it is the day breaking in all spaces. God is immanent in the universe, the miracle of creation is every moment repeated. Light is everywhere issuing from darkness; order from chaos. The kingdom of heaven is rising up clear, sweet, imperturbable, into the Divine Presence. The authority of this revelation is ample, the only ample authority—the fact that the earth and the heavens are meeting each other and embracing each other, in all the ministrations of life, through the whole stretch of vision.

We should understand how thoroughly the instruction of God is object-teaching. The world of facts lies under the world of ideas, its serene reflection, its stable form. If we are redeemed, saved, purified; redemption, salvation, purification are not dogmatic assertions, dull text, they are visible facts, brilliant illuminations, whose beauties we hourly experience. We cannot have a philosophy of life, a spiritual interpretation of life, which does not issue in life itself. Are Christians saved? And if so, how are they saved? These are most pungent and pertinent questions, and are to be answered on this side and on that, in inner force and outer form, in full view of the facts of the world and of the ideas regnant in it. History, with its vices, virtues, decay, reform, littleness and largeness of spiritual life, lies as a map before us, that we may find our own whereabouts, and our lines of march in the divine plan. He that has eyes to see, let him see; and he must see the clearest wisdom of God in the events that are nearest him, the foreground of his picture. Mirage, illusion, are always at play on the horizon. We must walk with the omniscience of God where that omniscience is most immediate to us, in our own lives. This is inspiration. If we put inspiration, as a gift, far back among the servants of God, we put it far off from our own thoughts. Our lives are the types of all lives, and should be richer than the lives of those who have gone before us, because we are higher up in the mount of vision.

Is then the truth, the truth which fills the universe of God, as a trumpet made for its proclamation; the truth which is the breath of every living spirit, the invisible presence that moves creatively on the face of the waters, that otherwise surge aimlessly and darkly in the social world; is then the truth so inferior and insufficient, that we need something other than it, called Revelation, to take its place, and do its work? Nay, indeed. Christ is the way and the truth and the life; and this life is the light of men, the true light that lighteth every man that cometh into the world. With him we abide livingly and lovingly among divine things. What God is to one he is to all, and, in a profound sense, equally to all. Our inspiration is the inspiration which God has poured out from the beginning, like sunshine and rain, for the fertilization of all fields, and whose creative touch we to-day enjoy as never before.

We accept then that view of inspiration which makes it stand for the normal hold of the human mind on truth, under all the liabilities and limitations which belong to its powers. In this process of truth-finding, truth-feeding, God is pre-eminently near us, helping our thoughts from within and from without; especially is he near to us in our approach to those higher truths which are revelations in the deeper world of spiritual being. We so earnestly and urgently reject the more familiar doctrine of inspiration, not because it does not aver for most minds a fact of great moment, but because it has come to be used as a key to a dogmatic structure, a wedge that, driven to its place, holds firm the entire edifice of theological thought; that greatly needs to be rebuilt by us. There is a lazy love of authority and finality that we all, more or less, share; but he who places his hand in the hand of God to be led of him must be up by times, take many weary steps, and find himself in many obscure places. Yet thus there is safety, and thus there is strength. We are ready to strive for this liberty, to walk with God.

It has been necessary to urge at length, and in the very outset, these difficulties of inspiration, because only thus could we be fully restored to naturalism, God's universal method of dealing with men, those safe, sober paths of thought and action in which he daily leads us. The doctrine of inspiration, standing at the entrance of inquiry into religious truth, settling its method, and assigning its peculiar tests, forbade any sound naturalism in faith, and threw the mind at once into a conflict with knowledge and the growth of knowledge, which spring from the deep, fertile soil of natural and spiritual law. We could not otherwise so much as open our inquiry, or open a way to it. The New Theology is involved in this very movement toward more breadth and more unity in all truth, this identification and integrity of method in all worlds.

If now we accept all truth as resting flatly and fully on its own laws, it may be thought that we have escaped one difficulty in harmonizing religion with nature only to encounter another and greater one. Can prayer also be made to stand on the basis of law? Are miracles only manifestations of uniform methods? We wish to give ourselves to no feats of interpretation, feats that overstrain and destroy the truth they are intended to present. Our naturalism is not a naturalism of physical laws simply. We do not in the least accept the dictum of Huxley that "the progress of science has in all ages meant, and now means more than ever, the extension of the province of what we call matter and causation, and the concomitant gradual banishment from all regions of human thought of what we call spirit and spontaneity." Quite the reverse of this, knowledge, wisdom seems to us to be the extension and reconciliation of both these primary terms of thought, till they interlace each other in every part of a universe that was dead and is alive.

Prayer is in harmony, wholly in harmony, with spiritual law. If there is any universal method which belongs to the feeble, dependent human mind, it is this method of asking and giving aid. So incorporate is prayer in the constitution of man, that he cannot but pray. He may close his lips, but his heart remains full of it, under any exigency. But if it is a law of mind to seek help, it must, with a theistic interpretation of the world, become a fixed portion of a rational method to bestow help. The asking and the receiving are complementary under one set of powers. If it is a law of mind to think, thought must be a factor in success. If it is a law of the affections to seek sympathy, it is equally a law to confer it. No construction of the spiritual world could be more unequal and incongruous than a prayerless one, or one of unanswered prayer. This would be to give and withhold in the same act; to confer powers, and repress their exercise. As a matter of fact, the affections owe a vigorous, free, enjoyable life to this very act of prayer. We must hold by things as they are. This is empiricism. It is no part of our philosophy to believe that the world is wholly different from that which it offers itself to us as being. We leave such conclusions to theorists.

But prayer, if it strengthens and sustains the mind, ought to find, and does find, entrance thereby into the physical world. As long as mind is a term of energy in that world, a mental effect may become a physical one; and prayer may be an agency whose action is present among physical events. Prayer is thus certain to extend at least an indirect influence over current circumstances.

Nor is it opposed to true naturalism to believe that prayer may meet with a direct answer in the modification of physical things. In the naturalism of the world, as we understand it, mental processes and powers hold a certain supremacy among physical forces. To understand the conditions of control, and control itself, is the very gist of naturalism. That God should aid wise endeavor, no more throws us off the basis of endeavor than does the response of our fellow-creatures to our petitions. Prayer may be used to weaken effort, and so may it be used to strengthen it. Wisely used, it leaves unaltered the laws of action,— the physical and spiritual naturalism which envelops it. It certainly marks a peculiar feature of that naturalism, and in that feature we supremely believe. It is not easy to overrate the force of sympathetic, spiritual life.

If it be said that prayer, as effecting direct results among physical things, is, if possible, incapable of proof, we at once demur. It is, indeed, incapable of sensuous proof, but not of proof. It is contrary to the conditions of the problem to demand sensuous proof. If the answer of prayer were established in this way, it would become a miracle; and a miracle stands in very different spiritual relations. Prayer subserves primarily a sympathetic, rational purpose. On that basis, there is ample evidence of the answer of prayer in the lives of many millions. On that basis, its answer must rest; for only thus can it reach its object of ministering to faith. To try to push it from its own pivot of revolution, and test it as a naked, physical fact, is to lift the magnetic needle from its rest, and still insist on its vibration. It is quite sufficient if physical events, rendered in a sensuous way, do not contradict the answers of prayer; the spiritual energy that accompanies them must always remain spiritual, as much so as the energy of mind.

So in turn the typical miracle, as the miracles of Christ, is wholly in keeping with naturalism. The miracles of our Lord are the highest expression of the fundamental fact of naturalism, the interpenetration of physical laws and mental processes, the triumph of reason through the entire realm of being. The miracles of healing were wrought under, not by, natural laws, and left those, so renovated, on precisely the same plane of physical forces on which it found them. The gifts of these miracles were chiefly spiritual. The physical gains were soon lost again, if the living impulse of divine love—an impulse so native to the highest development of the human spirit—was not felt. The miracle of help is no more abnormal, no more subversive of a true naturalism, coming on fitting occasion from the hand of God, than is the assistance by which one restores his neighbor, who has fallen in the road, to his feet.

The feeling of opposition between the wisely ordered miracle and natural law arises from the very narrow limits we put upon naturalism, as the uniformity of physical sequences, clamped close within themselves. Any modification of these mechanical terms is their breakage. Accept a true theism, a theism which puts personal reason—we say personal reason, though reason is the very essence of personality—at the very centre of all things; a theism which makes reason, as the cohesive law of thought, as wide as thought itself; a connection of creation as pervasive as creation itself, and there is no damage done the lower by the rule of the higher over it. When it prevails as uniformity, and when it prevails as an exception, the fact is equally one of reason. The miracle is only a more marked expression of a relation that is prevalent everywhere. The miracles of Christ aid us in comprehending the world; they do not alter its construction, or our permanent standing in reference to it. Instead of discord and disproportion, there are the highest harmony, the widest naturalism, the most manifest assertion of the most fundamental fact, the omnipresence of reason. What limits reason shall assign itself, is an empirical lesson of the Divine Reason addressed to the reason of man.

We have the firmest faith in naturalism, but no patience with a naturalism that takes the most narrow and inflexible term in our complex experience, and sets it up as the absolute type of all terms. We are pleading for the naturalism of reason, and not of causation built up by reason against itself. We refuse to chisel an idol, and then bow down to it. In a stony presence of this kind, all spiritual life is petrified. There is no iconoclasm in which we are more hearty than that which breaks down the images of the senses set up in the temple of reason. We believe in God, and the laws that he has framed cannot, beyond their own uses, stand against him. We accept reason, and all the claims of reason, but that reason should subject itself to its own products is not among these claims. The denial of the fitness of a miracle is the abrogation of reason in behalf of physical laws, when life has been allowed to sink out of them, till they have become the dead, inflexible, crust of things. Spiritual life in all its terms perishes under such a process. Reanimate law once more with the living reason it contains, and it regains at once flexibility and submits itself to all the uses of life.

It may still be felt that the inflexibility of physical law is a simple, well-established fact of experience, and that a fact cannot be pushed aside by a reason. But has this inflexibility been established? Certainly it has been established, as the fruit of reason, if it has been established at all. It is not a matter of sensation. The problem much transcends our experience. We are brought back then once more to reason, and it is just as much within the scope of reason to recognize the inflexibility of physical laws under purely physical terms and their flexibility under spiritual terms as it is simply to assert their absolute uniformity. We abide with reason, and we must have reasons, the gold currency of mind, for what is offered in the name of reason. All turns on the true key of thought in the world. We believe that reason unlocks itself and unlocks all things, that its law is within itself, that the final term in light is light itself. Mind, whose office is exposition, expounds both matter and mind. Matter, the relatively opaque and passive element, does not measure mind, the relatively transparent and active element. Mind cannot be allowed to perish in its own presence by its own processes in deference to conceptions that are its own creation.

The miracle, as the expression of the supreme term in the cosmos, may easily break bounds, has often broken bounds, in men's thoughts. But so may every trace of order, dependent on man's conception of it, be effaced or confused. Superstitions are the ugly, ravelled fringe of spiritual life. Life, the more extended it is in its field, the more delicate in its processes, is but the more liable to these miserable perversions of its own growth. In this relation the miracle is akin to what we find everywhere. We scale the heights of being by a complexity and balance of action of most unstable equilibrium, at the farthest possible remove from the stolid dependencies of mechanism. The checks and counter-checks of thought are not to discourage us by their multiplicity and subtilty, if we are to make ourselves heirs of the Infinite. Who can tell how the bird rides the wind, and who can sufficiently define the poise of the spirit between physical and spiritual things! When we consider the patience with which, in spite of all flutter and feebleness of wing, the mind of man has pushed, and is pushing, its way upward into the region of spiritual life, how empty of authority do the vigorous words seem by which Positivism represses this spirit, and bids it back again to the earth. "History will place your dogma in its class, above or below kindred competing dogmas, exactly as the naturalist classifies his species. From being a conviction it will sink into a curiosity; from being the guide to millions of human lives it will dwindle down into a chapter in a book. As history explains your dogma so science will dry it up; the competing law will silently make the conception of the daily miracle of your altars seem impossible; the mental climate will gradually deprive your symbols of their nourishment, and men will turn their backs on your system, not because they have confuted it, but because, like witchcraft or astrology, it has ceased to interest them."*

This passage vividly describes a most real movement, that by which the chaff is winnowed from the wheat—error eliminated from truth. But when the author expects to find only seed wheat, and all of it, in his own sieves, the totality of truth among his own convictions, we are astonished at the insight and the lack of insight which his words convey. We must have both the harvest of thought and the gleaning of all its fields before we can fill our granaries, and turn the key on our treasures. We have room for physical things, and room for spiritual things, and room for their mutual corrections; we have room for the gathering of the senses, and room for the touch of insight which turns it into the musical rhythm of thought. The wind with which John Morley proposes to clean our threshing-floor would prove a veritable cyclone driving away not the chaff, simply, but the grain of thought so

* John Morley, "Miscellanies," vol. i., p. 81.

far won in our intellectual culture. We must, indeed, admit the energies of reform; they will certainly force their own entrance, as intimated, but we must not allow them to reform away, nor will they reform away, the very substance of life to which alone they are made to minister. What men have been doing from the beginning, that, from the nature of the case, they must continue to do to the very end; though they may, indeed, do it in a more complete way. No subsoiling can be so deep as to plough the very ground from under us. Spiritual germs are waiting extension, not extermination.

All that we have now occasion to enforce is the simple fact, that there is not, necessarily, in the miracle any conflict with naturalism, as a law of rational action. The nature of the supernatural—for it has a nature—and its relation to naturalism remain to be considered.

But it may be said, if we believe so profoundly in the supernatural, why have we been so urgent in our attack on inspiration? How can two walk together, unless they are agreed? The supernatural element, retained in inspiration, puts constant suspension and harmful limitation on naturalism, on reason, on the growth of mind under its own laws. The instant the spirit strives to move forward, in the highest realm of thought, it encounters this dogma, and is often turned peremptorily back by it. The glass in which, with open face, we behold the glory of God, and are changed into the same image from glory to glory, is that habitual reflection of him which we know as naturalism. We object to the ordinary view of inspiration, not because it involves supernaturalism, but because it stands in obscure, perplexing, and misleading relations with naturalism, the coherent method of God. We exclude this dogma in the interests of a true reconciliation of the double terms of being.

CHAPTER II.

THE SUPERNATURAL.

THERE is no question of religious thought more difficult or more urgent than that involved in the nature and reality of the supernatural. We may dispense with this inquiry, as we may dispense with any inquiry, by a belief or an unbelief that only partially understands its own grounds. If, however, the world of facts and the world of spiritual experiences are to assume anything like a clear and consistent expression for us, we must settle in our minds the limits and relations of the natural and the supernatural.

Religion, in all its forms, has had and must have to do, and that very freely, with the supernatural. A faith without the supernatural—if we should still insist on calling it a faith—could gain no hold on the general mind. Religion ordinarily does mean, and ought to mean, our belief in personal, spiritual agents; our relation to the problem of spiritual life. If any belief short of this is called a religion, it is so called because it has taken the place of religion, and we wish to give it, in its difficult and unnatural position, what prestige and support we can. What especially distinguishes religious faith from all other forms of faith is, that it lays hold on an invisible personal element, and assigns it some part in the world, no matter how obscure and partial that part may be. Such personal powers are, from the very nature of the case, supernatural, and their devotees are only too ready to accept any supernatural manifestation of their presence.

No faith can properly be called a religion which does not introduce the mind to this invisible world. However we may choose to employ words, there is nothing plainer than that a belief which accepts invisible spiritual factors will be so distinct from one that denies them as properly to belong to a peculiar class. Religions all agree in this assertion, and differ among themselves only in the character and control of these superhuman beings. These spirits, one and all, are found in the closest affiliation with the supernatural, and when they manifest themselves through the natural, it is made thereby to stand in different relations from those we ordinarily recognize in it. It is infused with a power and employed for a purpose which quite transcend it as cosmic mechanism.

Religious thought is especially liable to drop into superstition, to become wayward and fantastic in belief, and dangerous and fanatical in action, at this point of supernatural intervention. No definition is, therefore, more urgent for religion itself than this which defines the relation of the visible and the invisible in the government of human life. This is the problem which every form of faith that aims in any degree to be rational must work over, again and again, in connection with our increasing knowledge of the world. It is time that the ignorance which once might have been winked at should pass away. The entire inductive growth of religious truth and life lies here. New methods, fresh corrections and restraints, are brought to belief by a better mastery of the natural, and a better apprehension of the limits it assigns the supernatural. Thus, on the practical and the theoretical side alike, the one thing to be correctly fathomed in faith, the one thing to be wisely applied in conduct, is the inner and abiding relation of spirit and form, substance and expression, the Divine Being and the divine mode of being. Is the form form through and through? Is the physical physical to its very core? Is the natural dead by means of laws that have no purpose or constructive idea; that neither arise, nor can carry the mind, beyond themselves? These are questions which reason, because of its own life, cannot fail to ask, nor can it fail to be profoundly affected by the answers given them. The religious tendency—a tendency native to thought—is always struggling for a supernatural something of the nature of spirit, which lies back of, above, and beyond, all the sensible terms of our experience.

The scientific tendency, later in its development, leads us to magnify the natural, and, in its extreme expression, to exclude with it the supernatural. The terms of exact knowledge lie chiefly in physical things and events, bound together as causes and effects. The extension of these relations is the expansion of determinate thought, and all the successes of the past century urge us to complete the work by giving full sweep to the ruling idea. This movement has, for the moment, gathered great momentum, and those who wish to put any restraints upon it, or supplement it by earlier forms of inquiry, are easily pushed aside, or looked upon as having scant claims even to this courtesy.

While there have arisen many secondary points of discussion between religion and science, points at which science has been more frequently in the right, the real difficulty of reconciliation between the two methods of thought is found in this very thing, the supernatural.

Science has an instinctive disrelish for the supernatural, as something in whose presence its own methods are of no avail, something from which there goes forth an obscuring, chilling mist of uncertainty, that brings inquiry speedily to an end. The supernatural, instead of being an essential term in a higher order, is felt to be a loss of all order in chaos and confusion. The controversy, therefore, between science and religion, our knowledge of the physical world and our knowledge of the spiritual world, can only be settled by a just definition of the natural and supernatural, and by a determination of their dependence on each other. If reason excludes either, we cannot know the fact too quickly; if both are to be gathered up in one universe, this is a primary truth in human knowledge.

It is hardly necessary to add that our successful handling of the world as a whole must turn on our reconciliation, either by exclusion, or by subordination, or by concurrence in a result more comprehensive than either alone can offer, of these two terms, form and spirit, matter and mind, the natural and the supernatural. We can in no other way reach the power and the peace of our own lives. The questions, What are the aims of life? Is life worth living? are so frequently raised, and so variously answered, because we have been losing the harmonious stroke of the two wings by which we rise, and ride on the impalpable atmosphere of the spiritual world. In consequence, we have revolved helplessly in it, or plunged fatally from it.

What then are the natural and the supernatural? If we can satisfactorily distinguish these two things in their own nature, we shall easily understand the part they play in the universe, and readily furnish the proof on which they rest. There is very general consent as to what is to be understood by the natural, in its narrow signification. It covers all things and events which are interlocked by causal relations—phenomena that are settled in their form and order of procedure. Every purely physical occurrence is completely conditioned by coëxistent and antecedent circumstances, and it is these fixed dependencies which constitute its nature. However variable this nature may seem to be, the appearance is deceptive, for all results are perfectly defined by the energies involved. Here is a conception so distinct and final as to claim, on our part, clear recognition. As to this central phase of the natural, there should be no confusion or doubt. It is a form of being without degrees and vanishing lines. The entire physical world conforms to the conception.

But do all events come under these unchangeable relations? Most assuredly not. To present at once the nearest and strongest example of another law, thought cannot be regarded as natural in this narrow meaning of the word. If it is, in any sense, natural, it is so in a higher and wider way. It is natural simply as provided for in the framework of things, and habitually associated with it, and not as itself a constituent term enclosed in it. This use of the word is so much more extended than the previous one, in the connections implied, that nothing but confusion can arise if we do not carefully mark the widening of meaning when we include both sets of facts under one term. It is fatal to the higher relations of thought to crowd them in with the lower ones of physical events; or it loosens the lower ones at once to include with them the wider phenomena. The essential connection, in the one case, is causation, and, in the other, that of spontaneous procedure under the laws of truth. The laws of truth are not involved as forces in facts, but imply the conformity of the mind, under its own insight, to the impalpable thought-relations of things. This conformity is established by the mind itself, and therefore the mind is and must be free in pursuing it. No search for truth, that is not deceptive, can be entered on without this spontaneous, self-directed movement. No conformity can be established between our conclusions and the facts to which they pertain without accompanying insight, and the action of the mind under it. If truth seems to elude us, we must be able to pursue it. If it is a certain something addressed to the mind alone, then the mind must have powers and laws—those of thought—in reference to it. All that declares human freedom declares also this special relation of thoughts within themselves. It is sufficient, however, to insist on one thing, and that one thing is so conclusive as to render absolutely inadmissible the extension of causation to all processes. To affirm that thoughts have the same causal relations as things is to destroy truth, and is, therefore, a self-destructive affirmation. If our judgments are interwoven with the forces that impel the physical world, with the fixed connections that control it, then each and every judgment, as a simple fact, must, like other facts, have a sufficient cause; and all judgments must have one and the same right to be, that of being; that of inclusion in the nature of things. No judgment can be opposed to any other judgment as true or false; all are equally real, equally the product of adequate causes, equally included in the framework of the world. If, as Huxley affirms, consciousness "is a function of nervous matter, when that nervous matter has attained a certain degree of organization," we shall be utterly unable to define that peculiar relation of thoughts—themselves subtile products of causation—to the other products of causation, which we term truth.

The distinction between the true and the false must disappear, and that between the real and the unreal take its place. If one strives to restore the conception of truth as the correspondence of judgments with the reality of things, he must mean by the reality of things, not the actuality of things,—for our thoughts are only the counterparts of the intellectual relations expressed by things, and never a reproduction of the things themselves, —but certain supersensible connections involved in them. But how involved? Certainly not as any form of phenomena, but only as the possible interpretation of the phenomena. This possibility is outside of causation, something put upon it by mind, and by mind alone. Here, then, we have a triple separation of the movement of thoughts from the movement of things. It is toward an idea and not toward an event—it is not the very act of thought, but the intellectual product of the thought, that interests us. This distinction of results lies in the realm of the true and the false, and not in that of the real and the unreal. The result itself is one of immediate, conscious conformity, and not one of prior, unconscious determination. The search for truth must be a conscious one, since truth is a visible agreement, under insight. Events, merely, gain nothing by consciousness, since the forces which settle them lie deeper than consciousness and are incapable of independent modification in it.

If mind is under natural, causal law, truth is three times lost. It is lost in fact, as the only question becomes one of realities. It is lost in theory, as there is nothing other than mere facts to which the thoughts, themselves mere facts, can conform. There are no additional facts, called truths, to which the process of development can bend. And truth, if granted in theory, is lost in attainment, since we can give no reason why a series of thoughts produced by one series of causes should conform to a series of relations expressed by other facts, under their own independent lines of causation. Causes can only reach facts, and those of a predetermined order. Truths must themselves be phenomenal characteristics, if they are to be included in phenomena; while the method of coincidence remains entirely unintelligible.

We must stanchly deny, therefore, that thoughts are causal, contained in nature, in its limited sense. They are rather, in their origin, supernatural; since they play upon nature from above for its interpretation in physical and spiritual uses. Their laws are laws of their own, and their conformity to them is achieved by a higher impulse than physical forces.

If we look at the way in which the two terms, thoughts and things, are united, the same conclusion is forced upon us by another method. This junction is accomplished by intervention of the brain. The processes which take place in this highly organized organ, an organ which contains the most delicate, varied, complex, mobile, and dependent forms of activity anywhere found in the physical world, are purely physical, and have their types in methods elsewhere present. Brain action presents a closed circle of forces that run through a familiar circuit within themselves. The energies that are realized in decomposition are expended in motion, heat, recomposition. There is in this expenditure no known term that takes the form of thought or feeling. These are incidents, not facts, of the process. Thought has no phenomenal expression which it can take, side by side with physical activities. No one of these is the equivalent of thought, transmutable into it, or capable of being restored from it. Thought remains a perfectly intangible accompaniment of these tangible terms. Brain constituents, in their consumption, do not give it, nor can it return to the 'form of these constituents. On the other hand, these issue in their own equivalents, wholly aside from thought. In discussing brain action within its own circle of composition and decomposition, we have no more occasion to consider thoughts and feelings beyond the nervous activity incident to them, than we have, in making up the product of expenditures in a steam-engine, to estimate the play of shadows; or the mind of the operator in computing the waste of a telegraphic circuit.

Thought does attend, or may attend, on these physical activities, complete within themselves in the brain and body of man. The amount of thought will stand in close relation to the volume of movement, but the nature of thought as thought will not determine the nature of the nervous activity, nor the nature of the nervous activity decide that of the thought. Slow, inaccurate, and perplexed thinking will consume brain energy as certainly as rapid, correct, and ready apprehension. Thought on one subject will involve essentially the same changes—not perhaps absolutely identical ones in the parts of the brain affected— as thought on a very different subject. The divisions of thought, so far as they reappear in distinctions of nervous action, do it under perfectly disparate terms. What is a mental difference here is a local one there. The brain thus takes, in reference to the mind, the position of an instrument which both limits and aids the mind, and has many degrees of aptness in reference to it. Yet it no more determines the direction and perfection of execution than do the tools of the carpenter the form and success of his work.

The superior and supersensible relation of the mind, in spite of the closeness and constancy of its dependence on the brain,—yet not closer or more constant than that of the telegrapher on his instrument—is anticipated and typified in that intermediate term between matter and mind which we call life. It is not merely brain, but the living brain, which is the organ of thought. So unable have those been, who are striving to give a fixed interpretation, under physical forms, to all parts of the world, to find any satisfactory exposition of life, or place for it in their system, that some of the most able and sharp-sighted of them all, like Professor Huxley, have denied its existence as an entity of any sort. The physical terms of the living thing are complete within it, and fully cover the phenomena before us. Life finds no place among them as one of them. It is thought, therefore, to be an unwarranted act of mind to create for it another position on another plane, above them or back of them, and enthrone it thereon as a supersensuous presence. The living circle, sufficient unto itself, needs only itself for its comprehension.

By this method of thought the very notion of comprehension, the reference of phenomena to something deeper than themselves, is set aside. Each step in the dance is a simple mechanical fact; the entire dance is made up of these distinct steps, therefore the form and rhythm of the whole are sufficiently covered by the exposition of the parts. It is possible to say this in reference to life, because life declares itself only in and by these intertwined circuits of molecular and atomic movement, this dance of the elements. It is not possible to say it in reference to mind,

—though exactly the same reasons lead us to wish to say it—because the wholly distinct phenomena of mind in consciousness declare the presence of something in addition to all physical facts. Yet these mental phenomena find no more place among the physical terms which accompany them, than does life among organic functions. In both cases, a result addressed to the mind, is made the ground of inferring a corresponding agency.

If we hold that a certain series of physical facts manifest themselves in an additional way as a series of mental phenomena, we must also hold, under the notion of causation, that these phenomena are the expression of those physical forces, and stand on terms of transfer with them. Not only are these conclusions subversive of the very nature of truth, and therefore to be summarily rejected by the truth-loving temper, they find no confirmation in our knowledge of nervous facts, and bring no light to our thinking. It is as impossible to discover thought in the brain economy, as it is impossible to pick up life in our anatomy of physical organs. Thought may easily enough be said to be a specific, higher form of life. Yet these heroic assertions we have chosen to make not only sweep aside the habitual methods of mind, they do nothing whatever for us, unless it be regarded a solution of the problem to abolish the problem itself; an explanation of differences to deny their existence.

If the distinctive phenomena of life do not establish life as a real agent, then the peculiar phenomena of mind do not give us mind as a spiritual entity. Thus mental activity sinks at once into a mere succession of phenomena. Our earnest affirmations, our sharp denials, our indignation, our ardent vindication, are either mere appearances, or are determined by something quite other than themselves.

If there were the least philosophy left in us by such a philosophy, which there well enough may not be, we should be content simply to watch these shadows of clouds pursuing each other across the intellectual landscape. We must, then, start our philosophy with the validity of truth; and this is found only in the integrity of the mind itself, in the coherence and justness of its own processes, in the essential soundness of knowledge.

Here, then, in mind, we have something obviously supernatural; indeed, the very term which leads us to entertain the notion of the supernatural, and make use of it in our processes of thought. What can be a better image of the supernatural, something above nature, as a closed circuit, and in free use of it in spite of its closure, than mind? An engineer is watching his engine in reference to correction. When he shall strike in, how he shall strike in, whether he shall strike in at all, are points he is waiting to determine. Whatever change he makes, takes its appropriate place in the circle of physical conditions, and the outcome of them all is altered by it. This involves a supernatural presence, not a power detached from the natural and alien to it, not a power included within the natural and bound by it, but a power that from its own resources works on and through the natural, and by its labor brings forth within the natural fresh returns for itself. The moment the inquirer recognizes the truth-seeking, truth-obeying processes for what they are, he holds the secret of the supernatural.

Confusion frequently arises in the discussion of evolution because of the different degrees of force which are assigned the word. It may imply that each succeeding state is wholly included in the preceding one, or only that they are closely united to each other, the former with its full quota of work passing into the latter. A narrower and a wider meaning, in a similar way, attach to naturalism. We may mean by it conclusively causal relations, or we may include in it the whole empirical system of which we are a part, with its intellectual as well as its physical terms. When, in our first chapter, we affirmed naturalism, we expressly gave it this wide meaning; now, when we contrast it with supernaturalism, accepting the latter also, we assign it its narrower signification. It is not easy to avoid the double use, because it is involved in the double character of the facts themselves. There is in it no confusion of thought, and need not be of presentation, if the attention is distinctly drawn to it. Intellectual activity lies between purely causal and purely spiritual forms of being, and is affiliated with both. As provided for by fixed physical conditions, it is natural; as active within itself under impulses of its own order, it is supernatural. The unity of the natural and the supernatural, the rationality of both forms of being, is achieved by the intervention of this common term.

When one is occupied with pure thought, he abides in a spiritual region; when he contemplates the conditions of action under thought, or its concomitants, he enters the realm of causation.

We have three things to consider: physical, causal facts; intellectual, empirical facts; purely spiritual, supersensuous phenomena—such as we attribute to God. The second term lies between the other two,—the natural and the supernatural—and will be united now to the one and now to the other according to the manner in which we contemplate it. Intellectual activity as associated with definite physical conditions is natural, a part of the system of nature; as within itself a law to itself, and so acting from above on nature, it is supernatural. Two conical hills may lie so near each other that the base of the one deeply intersects the base of the other. Neither can be completely constructed without including material which belongs to the other. If we cut down arbitrarily between them we mutilate both. It is by this constant over-lap that the continuity of the world is preserved. In man two kingdoms meet, and from this central position we must be able to pass out either way.

The totally distinct things, on the relation of which all interpretation depends, are physical facts, whose character is determinate and fixed; and pure spiritual processes, ready, by a predetermination that arises within themselves, to pass into external expression. Man, as a truly intellectual and free being, deals with both these elements. Freedom implies both, implies the outward limitation which conditions activity, and the inner intellectual life which determines it. We may, for purposes of expression, annex this realm of freedom, so deeply immersed in physical relations, to nature; or we may, for purposes of exposition, unite it to those ever-abiding supernatural energies from which it derives its pre-eminent characteristics.

The natural and the supernatural so meet in mind, so flow together in the events of a rational universe, as not only to leave no conflict between them, but to make them everywhere the woof and warp of one web. When we reach the deepest thing in causal relations it turns out to be an intellectual dependence.

It would be fortunate if we were able to give a distinct designation to each of the three things with which we have to deal; events moving necessarily forward under physical dependencies; the rational acts of men self-directed under the conditions which enclose them; and the absolute activities of God, which assign to themselves both directions and conditions. The word natural covers the first; the word supernatural applies with least confusion to the third alone. We are thus left with no reciprocal designation of the intermediate, uniting term, the voluntary movements of men; coining a word, we may call these internatural. They start in nature, they terminate with nature; but they themselves are not included parts of it. The supernatural is thus left as the exclusive designation of that which lies above nature and acts upon it constructively. Whether we accept these three terms, or shuffle on with a double service assigned to the supernatural, we shall not clearly apprehend the subject till these distinct forms of activity are perfectly before us. The true connection of the natural and the supernatural is found in the internatural. This alone unites them in a system.

One mystery makes all these plain, and familiar facts obscure to some minds, the mystery of contact between the spiritual and the physical. But this mystery—if it be wise to call it one—is the exact mystery of the ultimate, wherever and whenever we reach it, the mystery of gravitation, of cohesion, of chemical affinity. It is always by accepting one mystery that we make many mysteries plain. Reason, insight, lie just here in accepting ultimates wisely; and one ultimate in itself is as plain as another. When an act becomes single, it thereby becomes simple. It admits of no analysis and no explanation. When things so distinct as spiritual phenomena and physical phenomena affect each other, an intermediate, as a term of exposition, becomes absurd. It doubles the mystery. It renews the error so long persisted in of expounding vision by an emanation from the thing visible.

The relation of man, as a finite being, to nature, is necessarily distinct from that of God as an infinite being. The natural is foreign to man, something which proceeds without him, and is approached by him only in narrow and carefully ordered ways. This path of approach is his own physical organization. Each living thing has its own terms of mastery, less broad or more broad, over physical forms. All lives, taken collectively, penetrate the physical elements in innumerable ways for innumerable uses, and stand up, in and by each other, in a wide command of the world. All this service, by virtue of his superior and more complex endowments, culminates in man. That slow, organic development, therefore, by which, as the latest and highest form of life, he gathers up the reins of power which have been placed in his hands, and guides the world for his own spiritual purposes, is doubly the condition of his control. His manifold physical endowments are the immediate terms in this government; and like endowments, as varied and multiplied in all lives, at a second remove, minister to his purposes, and rest his power deeply and broadly on the soil of the earth.

This evolution, also, carries with it the ability to comprehend the world, and opens backward to him the years of God. The intellectual stratum, on which his activity rests, is as deep as the physical stratum, and at one with it. The natural is that world of substantial, completed thought with which his finite powers, in their unfolding, are united, and into which they go forth. Here they find both the conditions and limits of activity. The natural and the supernatural are in equipoise in man, are alike the terms of his life. The natural is the conduit of his supernatural power which bounds it, guides it, and gives way before it. The world is serviceable in the degree in which it is intelligible. It is intelligible, when considered as holding these two constituents, in a far more profound and comprehensive fashion than when looked on in any other manner. This is the way in which men, by the growth of knowledge, have come more and more to understand the dependencies of matter and mind. These two terms, the natural and the supernatural, are the banks between which their thoughts have always flowed, and are still flowing. Efforts to lift them out of these familiar channels must be unsuccessful, because they are opposed to the gravitation of mind. We might as well expect to turn all the waters of the world into aërial ways. As mind has thus far asserted itself, so it will continue to assert itself. It cannot accept, and it never will accept, conclusions at war with its own processes and its own powers. Knowledge with man means a certain mastery of mind over matter, and this it will continue to mean. His power to modify the world for future uses turns on this relation. Things are changeable and lives are variable in his hand, and so he multiplies the ministrations of the world to himself. The sense of this control not only can not depart from man, it is constantly on the increase. The growth of knowledge, instead of limiting the supernatural, is continually adding to its scope as rightly understood. We are perpetually passing from physical laws to personal powers, from personal powers to physical laws, in the rhythm of intellectual and spiritual progress.

The natural alone is a flinty rock on which nothing can be grown, out of which nothing can be cut; the supernatural alone is shifting clouds which dissolve and redissolve in meaningless forms. The natural, flexible under the supernatural, is the marble chiselled into the statue, is the opening flower built together by the fugitive light and brooding moisture. The natural and the supernatural are different sides of the same thing, the earthward and the heavenward side, the outer and the inner side. When we walk in the light of our intuitions and affections, we are most touched by a sense of the Divine Presence; when we take counsel and put our hands to work shrewdly on the things about us, we are most impressed by law, by stubborn conditions, by the slowly yielding material into which human and divine thoughts transform themselves.

God and man, if they are to meet in activity at all, and the overshadowing attributes of the one feed, without engulfing, the feeble faculties of the other, must find a middle term which shall be the hiding of the Divine Presence, on the one side, and the drawing out of human powers, on the other side. Nature is such a middle term. God here meets us, makes terms with us, gives us our lessons, and assigns us our tasks. So disciplined there are two suppositions we can make, equally false, equally productive of indolence and irresponsibility. We may magnify the natural, and say that this apparent potency of ours is all deceptive. That, in some subtle way, nature overrules us, and runs around us, and drives us about in a meaningless manner. Or we may magnify the supernatural, and regard the present terms of life as arbitrary, to be shaken off, as they have been imposed, by the divine will. We may thus wait for new developments, as if the law of change were simply one of fortuitous connections. The one is the error of an undue extension of causal relations, the other the error of magnifying voluntary dependencies. They are equally opposed to that coherent movement of reason by which thought, with no loss of its own fluency, is forever passing into the framework of things.

The natural, then, is that completed product of spiritual activity which expresses itself in things, events, actions, under law; and the supernatural is that spiritual potentiality, present both in man and God, which is the source of nature. The one is form and the other is spirit.

The relation of man to nature, as enclosed in it and limited by it, readily leads him to misconceive God's relation to it. An exterior existence and control, akin to that of man, are assigned to God also. Some even ask for the brain of God, the point at which his lines of power converge. Such a connection of mind with matter is necessarily a finite one. The world, the instrument of mind, lies exterior to mind, to be subjected to such processes of life as are possible to mind, by means of its own physical organism.

The Infinite must act centre-wise, in a way not illustrated by man's control of nature. The thought of the world is inseparable from the energies of the world, in their forms, measures, and relations. The mind of God, if present at all, is present in them in their very inception, in their every manifestation. An incomplete symbol of this relation is found in the connection of the spirit and body of man. The control which the mind has over its own bodily organs is much more perfect and independent than that which it has over other things. Will, simple spiritual activity, carries with it ready responses within the circuit of the body, and realizes itself at once in physical results which cost the spirit nothing. A mind that thus sustained and increased at pleasure all physical forces in the entire compass of being would be infinite. The regularity of its action would give the laws of nature, and the natural would be the habitual expression of the supernatural. The two would be the form and force of the same thing. They might easily fall apart in our consideration of them, as the text of an author and the spirit of an author separate themselves in criticism, but the fundamental coherence of the two would still remain the all inclusive and ultimate fact.

Suppose this to be the relation of the physical world to God, that it is simply the Divine Mind presenting itself in a legible form, would the laws of nature, the causal connections of events, find place in it? We answer the question as we answer all like questions, on the basis of reason. We answer it, keeping step with the naturalist, when he says these laws are universal. Why? because any other supposition does not tally with the claims of reason. Is then a causal dependence of physical phenomena a rational one, if these phenomena rest back on mind? Evidently it is a rational one, as it addresses itself to the mind and government of man as no other connection could do. If facts are to be intelligible and manageable, they must have these dependencies which make them so.

Does this fact compel us to regard these connections as absolute? Not in the least. We admitted them as the expression of reason and in its service, and we cannot allow them to shake off that service. A method that becomes absolute thereby becomes arbitrary. A rule that can never be set aside brings its own distinct evils. Reason, the highest reason, does not allow itself to be held in subjection by its own processes, does not suffer the conditions of one form of structure to rule those of another. Reason is infinitely flexible and productive within itself. Reason, therefore, prepares us to expect more than one method, one manifestation of the supernatural, that each manifestation shall be subject to its own purposes, and that all shall be harmonized in the most varied uses of mind. It is fit that the supernatural which expresses itself in causal relations in the physical world should, in subserving other ends, transcend these relations.

The form most conspicuous and undeniable in which the supernatural manifests itself is the miracle. Much is unwisely said about the miracle as a violation of natural law. The word is intended to carry a sense of injury done to the constructive processes of the world. In the same spirit a martinet gives rightfulness to a rule aside from the purposes it is subserving. If the coherence of physical laws is the expression of reason, this elasticity under spiritual pressure may be equally so. The additions and subtractions of a miracle are not in conflict with the ends of law, they simply enlarge them. Nor are these additions and subtractions new in kind. They are the same in kind. If the sick are healed, they are healed by a reinforcement of natural forces. The Infinite is in no way bound beyond his own purposes to a given, quantitative expression. More or less rests on precisely the same power that rules at the familiar, medium mark. This alleged conflict, either of purpose or of method, disappears under any comprehensive reference of the world to reason. If the world contains no inherent reason, then reason can say nothing about it beyond vision ; but if it contains reason, then reason, in its full variety of method, must be conceded.

If we are to entertain the supernatural successfully, we must do it broadly, freely, as fulfilling a very general, harmonious, and concurrent purpose in creation. This it does as now offered. The supernatural, underlying everywhere the natural, declares itself distinctly in the development of life, and still more in rational spirits. The relation of spiritual life to physical things is one permeated with a supernatural element. It rises distinctly above the plane of causes. Under the guidance of these facts, we are able to find The Supernatural, the centre and life of all things, and are prepared for an explicit disclosure of this supremacy, on fitting occasion, in the miracle. It is the supposed irrationality of the miracle that precludes its acceptance by many; it is only its plain rationality that can make way for it again in the thoughts of all.

Huxley says that the rationalist no longer objects to the miracle as impossible, but as not sufficiently proved. But the proof is rejected chiefly because of the great, antecedent improbability which is supposed to attach to a miracle. Allow it to be an orderly factor in the spiritual world, and the historic proof, as in the narrative of our Lord, is quite sufficient to sustain it. If it is a term not of order but of confusion, no evidence will long avail. The thoughts of men everywhere, in belief and unbelief alike, set toward construction. This is the profound, the ruling, force in human knowledge.

In our time it is not the miracle that establishes the divine government, so much as it is the divine government that establishes the miracle. The supernatural is by no means that fragmentary, alien thing it is often conceived to be. If it were, we could not be too quickly rid of it. On the other hand, rightly understood, it is the very substance and soul of spiritual life, a life which is the inspiration of all being. The natural is to be swallowed up in the supernatural, or rather the two are inseparably to pervade each other, as the double terms of one creative process. Force and form abide together in all art.

The life of Christ is a far more complete fact, a more perfect integer, with the miracles than without them. It is almost impossible to pluck away, thread by thread, these supernatural connections and save any cohesive force or beauty in the fabric. The world with the life of Christ is a far more rational, a far more invigorating, thing than it is without that life. The reason, moving toward the higher ends of spiritual comprehension, finds need of this supreme fact, and, therefore, for the deepest of all reasons, gives it ready admission. Our thought, by means of it, makes full the circle of its own relations.

Let us take, without resting our argument wholly on it, the resurrection of our Lord as a favorable example of a supernatural event. Notwithstanding the confusion of the narratives, notwithstanding the greater difficulty which arises from the incongruity of the recorded events, some of them resting on a sensuous experience and some of them transcending it, some of them amenable to touch and vision and some of them not, we still believe it more rational to accept the fact of a resurrection than to deny it. The proof is sufficient to force the subject before the mind and to render any solution of it on a natural basis unsatisfactory. Many and momentous events seem to take their origin from it, and cannot well be explained without it. The highest spiritual congruity is attained by means of it. However perplexed we may be by the conflict of other considerations, this last consideration of spiritual congruity restores the equilibrium of the mind in firm belief. If we reject the event, on what ground shall we do it? Undoubtedly on the basis of the integrity of nature, the rational coherence of physical events. That is to say, those convictions of mind which find satisfaction in the constructive relations of natural agents predetermine us against this event as supernatural. But does not this same concession to reason in another direction and a higher one call for the acceptance of the resurrection? If we believe in a spiritual universe, as all our most penetrative insights compel us to, then is not the integrity, the inner sufficiency, of these spiritual convictions to have as much power with us as like considerations in connection with physical events? Certainly we shall not do well to allow one conclusion of mind to pull down others of equal or greater scope. The right by which the mind builds up the realm of natural law is in no way superior to that by which it compacts together the spiritual universe. One rational process is at the bottom of both of them. It is absurd for the mind to attach, by its own bent, such weight to physical considerations as to break down the cohesive force of its own higher movements. If it is entitled to the universality of physical law in a physical realm, it is equally entitled to the universality of spiritual relations in a spiritual universe.

We feel, therefore, that the world as a whole is more rational, more comprehensible, taken up into a higher unity, with than without the resurrection. We thus stand, as mind always stands, by faith, faith in its own processes, faith in the inner reason of things. That to which we direct attention in calling out this faith is the more sufficient and comprehensive way in which the universe, natural, internatural, and supernatural, is bound together by the resurrection. If we lose any one of these three terms, we lose a portion of the meaning of the other two; and the resurrection helps us to the meaning of them all. The meaning of the world is what we are seeking for, and if we do not know this meaning when we find it, our search must necessarily be futile.

But this conclusion is not so simple, looked at from all positions, as we may now seem to have made it. The mind that is long occupied with physical inquiries derives from them a tendency, very valuable and just within its own limits, but one that easily leads, first to the oversight, and then to the denial, of the spiritual phenomena of the world. The field of one engaged in physical research is too remote from these mountain summits, and, losing sight of them, he comes to disbelieve in them. The things nearest him contradict the alleged freedom of thought, and the continuity of the world seems at war with it.

Natural laws, to those who investigate them, assume a very absolute and universal form. This universality is emphasized at every stage of inquiry, and comes, at length, to be accepted as the primary fact in the world, and the first principle in philosophy. All knowledge is made to rest upon it. Certainly no man is prepared to carry on physical inquiries successfully who is not thoroughly possessed of this notion of causation. This is the lesson of the last hundred years. But when mind is regarded as subject to the same law, we are extending our induction into a new field, and that, too, with no revision of our premises, no new weighing of the facts. To assert causation here because it prevails elsewhere is to fall at once into *a priori* reasoning. To say that conclusions, logically coherent within themselves, owe their connection to certain prior physical dependencies, is to do in a new form, and in an opposite direction, what was so often and so unsuccessfully done in physics, when physical dependencies were expounded as mental ones, and nature was thought, like mind, to prefer and to abhor certain states and acts. Indeed, if we are not now in error in making acceptance and rejection in man the result of accompanying physical facts, the naturalists of a previous time were not so very much astray in thinking that a feeling, itself a phase of a physical state, might be a link in material connections.

We most assuredly need to remember that when we make the natural, in the form of causal relations, universal, we are proceeding simply on a presumption of mind, and in no way on direct, perceptive knowledge. The question between those who accept, and those who deny, the supernatural is one simply of reasonableness in method, of the soundness of that sweep of mind by which we go beyond the facts before us. The strict naturalist must subject all activities, even the activities on which the entire explanatory process depends, to physical law. Causation thus passes into mental phenomena and subdues them to itself. This conclusion, which stands at the threshold of strict naturalism, is, as already urged, one absolutely impossible to sound thought, since it destroys the very nature of thought. More than this, causes determine the mind to their own universal extension, and so the extension itself ceases to be a thing of reason and remains simply an insoluble fact. But it is not a uniform fact, since the majority of men reach no such conclusion. There is thus conflict and confusion in the facts, and there is no reason left us wherewith to correct them, to harmonize them with each other.

The second step of strict naturalism is somewhat less difficult, though still very difficult. It is the reference of the relations of things, completely intelligible, to something less than intelligence. The wisdom of the world—great as it is—is a water-mark within its own fibre. It enters into the very structure of things, and so shows that their putting together was a rational process. This naturalism must deny. It cannot admit that construction, like significant speech, rests on a meaning beneath it; that order is the product of wisdom and ruled by it; that nature reposes on the supernatural, which floats it as the ocean floats the vessel.

A third much easier denial of naturalism is that of the present modification of physical events by a divine agency. It denies the efficacy of prayer. Here unbelief has to do, not with the general interpretation of facts, but with the existence of certain specific facts. It seems, therefore, possible, at first sight, to bring the question in discussion to a practical test. Are there any answers to prayer? Many reply, Yes; and some reply, No. Can these discrepancies of opinion be brought to a rational settlement? Certainly not, if we mean by such a settlement one independent of our varying methods of interpretation; one equally satisfactory to all. The answer to prayer appeals to the mind of the supplicant. However much beyond the simply physical forces involved the answer of prayer may seem to have been, it can still be referred to these forces, and will be so referred by every one whose attitude of mind is such as to make such a reference seem more probable than the notion of divine aid. That is to say, in our explanations of the facts of the world which touch our dependence on God, we are merely giving a specific application of previous convictions, and we cannot maintain special cases without the general principles under which they are marshalled. It is every way unreasonable to expect the particular to stand up and contradict the general to which it belongs.

A belief in the answer of prayer arises in connection with an interpretation of facts, very wide and varied in character, and of very different degrees of force. Antecedent reasons are present with many minds which make the conclusion in a high degree probable. Facts seem to them to conform in a remarkable degree to this theory of the universe. Extreme naturalism, on the other hand, is so prepossessed against the expositions of faith, that it ridicules the less obvious examples of the answer of prayer, and disbelieves the more obvious ones. Affirmation and denial, on either side, have no absolute force. Proof is not a thing of vision, but turns on the constructive ideas we have recognized in the framework of things. No man can allow secondary, outstanding facts to contradict fundamental relations. This would be to yield the greater to the less, and undo all the work of thought.

If we were to establish two hospitals, as nearly as possible alike in their appliances and methods; if we were to govern the one by the temper of naturalism, and the other by that of faith,—a thing impossible to do in this predetermined fashion—doubtless the results would be somewhat different in the number of cures effected. Suppose this difference to lie on the side of faith, it would still be quite possible to say, and from the position of naturalism rational to say, that faith is itself a potent natural factor; that it gives enthusiasm and hope to those who entertain it, and so, as awakened life, becomes a restorative agency; that it imparts peace and resignation to those who suffer, and is thus a spiritual anodyne to physical irritations that otherwise exhaust the resources of life; in short, that the mind itself is an important factor in critical forms of disease, and that in these, its remedial relations, it is greatly strengthened by faith.

On the other hand, it would be equally possible to say that these results of faith imply the validity of faith, and rest upon it; that we cannot maintain enthusiasm, hope, peace, for a series of years in a series of minds, with no sufficient foundation for them; that this admitted efficacy of faith involves a sufficient reason, and that this reason is recognized by religion and denied by unbelief. These responses, backward and forward, would owe their force to prior principles, and would settle nothing independently of them.

The notion of a sufficient test of the efficacy of prayer is gross and irrational. It is gross because it implies that some visible and undeniable fact can be evidence of an invisible relation. We might with equal fitness demand of those who accept life as a plastic power, that it should be made tangible to us. It is irrational, because sound thought requires that we should give any alleged phenomena the precise conditions under which they are said to occur. We cannot do this in prayer in the form of an experiment. The mind cannot thus be left alone with God. We are virtually trying to quiz the spirit of man and the Spirit of Truth in their dealings with each other.

In the fourth place mere naturalism must deny—a denial easy in itself—the miracle. The test, just referred to, of visible results, should be applied to the miracle—if applied at all—and not to the answer of prayer. The answer of prayer always offers itself under a natural form, while the miracle transcends natural law in a bold and decisive way. But Hume was quite right in affirming that the miracle, on the basis of mere naturalism, cannot be established, even by vision. The miracle is one experience contradicting a thousand other experiences. There must be in the mind that accepts it some prior reason which reconciles the result with its previous knowledge, or belief in it is irrational. If I accede to one man's testimony against a thousand, there must be some other reason for this concession than the mere fact that he is one of the thousand. A single circumstance cannot contradict a hundred others resting on the same basis with it. The universality of causation, the one undoubted principle of knowledge, compels the man who accepts naturalism to believe, in the case before him, that sufficient causes are present to secure the anomalous result; and thus that result, whatever it is, ceases to be a miracle.

If miracles are rational, the historical proof is sufficient to make way for them; but if they are irrational, the historical proof weakens at once. This evidence is also further burdened by the fact that in the great majority of cases the alleged miracle is irrational, and so fails. The handling of proof turns constantly on intrinsic fitness.

What miracles, if any, are to be accepted, is a question to which we can make answer only when we have searched our philosophy through and through for the reasons of miracles. Miracles, whatever else they are or are not, are a supreme test of our methods of thought, the balance we have instituted between spiritual and physical energies. The works and words of Christ make an incomparable whole, a seamless garment. For this reason we believe in them with unwavering faith, but we can justify that faith only as the summation of all thought, as our deepest insight into the coherence of things.

Christ, it is said, did not many mighty works there because of their unbelief. As theologians often look at the miracle, this reason would seem to be unsound. The purpose of the miracle is thought to be the silencing of unbelief. So Elijah used it against the priests of Baal. The method of Christ implies that it is primarily a revelation of God to minds prepared to receive it. The miracle is not an assault on the gates of unbelief, an effort to carry the world by storm. This is profoundly impossible. It is a transfiguration, a melting of the visible before the eye of faith into the invisible, an overleaping of the limits of the visible with the glories of the invisible, a suffusion of lines in a marvellous play of light, art transcending itself.

If we are at all right in what we have said, the usual order of denial and affirmation must necessarily be barren of results. The root of the supernatural is not the miracle. This is at best the perfume of its topmost flower. That by which it roots itself in the earth, and holds it as its own, is the power of mind, the very nature of spirit. Naturalism, in the limited meaning in which we are now using the word, having weakened our sense of our own distinctive nature, is ready to deny the miracle, then to doubt the efficacy of prayer, then to swallow up the thought of the world in the inherent relations of material forces, and, in confirmation of all, to affirm the absolute oneness of law in matter and mind.

The proper line of defence in faith is the reverse of this. We must first understand the nature of spirit, human and divine—the law of mind within itself. We shall then see its relation to physical things, its flow through them, its transcription of itself in them as a visible medium of expression and a determinate field of action; the reserve of itself to itself by which, on occasion given by reason, it transcends the ordinary restraints of reason, and discloses itself by a light that, for an instant and for an instant only, darkens all other light.

If we consent to settle this question of the supernatural at the point of miracles, its most remote manifestation, with all the illusions against us which crowd in from the manifold superstitions of men, and with an overshadowing sense of the majesty of law as the full expression of the Divine Mind, we shall make concessions that we cannot recall, and find ourselves slowly pushed backward, till we have come under that great horror, instinctive and rational, life that is losing itself.

It is this faintness of the spirit within itself that, in works of fiction well conceived, makes the loss of faith so pathetic. The patient, under the slow inroads of unbelief, yields one and another disclosure of the supernatural, finds the miracle increasingly out of sorts with the historic world, finally turns to that world as one unbroken stretch of causal relations, and, if still earnest, enters on the despairing effort of restoring to itself and to others a spiritual presence. He inevitably fails in the effort, not because it is not a most needful one, but because the mind has too long been busy in chipping away every foothold and plucking up every shrub by which it might, like a wrecked mariner, mount the face of the cliff that now rises a sheer precipice before it. Such a one cannot fall back successfully on the inner testimony of the spirit, because, in painfully discrediting each of the manifestations of the spiritual history of the world, he has hidden much of that history from himself. Pre-eminently is this true for the popular mind. The preacher who is trying to persuade men to righteousness, conceiving it in its most abstract form, finds himself making violent, spasmodic efforts to breathe in an atmosphere too high and rare for the purposes of life, too high and rare for those whom he struggles to lead, by this remote and visionary path, into the experiences of faith. Heroism is all that remains to him.

This question of naturalism and supernaturalism can be safely settled only by a wide survey of the entire field. Assert distinctly the primitive powers of mind, and we are borne on by them till the world is everywhere the medium and expression of thought. Deny spiritual intervention in physical things, and one support after another of the personal element gives way, till the weary spirit, like a spent swimmer, sinks beneath the cold, restless surge of material forces. We should refuse to close an argument of this depth and moment until we have fully measured all its implications.

A whip, skilfully constructed, is completely elastic at one extremity and almost wholly inelastic at the other. The quality grows in one direction and declines in the opposite, and this it is which makes of it a perfect and graceful instrument. Inelastic throughout, and it is a cudgel, with which to bruise and to maim. The world is an admirable construction for the uses of mind, because inflexible physical and flexible spiritual forces interpenetrate each other everywhere in it. Try to understand it otherwise, make it rigid with natural law, and it becomes a club with which to beat the spirit and destroy its life.

The first purpose subserved by the supernatural is that of enabling us fully to understand the personifying tendency in man. We encounter this effort to penetrate to a personal core of things equally in sound thought and in earnest feeling. The world constantly reflects us to ourselves, and we are no longer alone in it. Face makes answer to face, as in a glass, and the mind of man awakens in a world of mind. There is no tendency in man more universal and irresistible than this tendency to seek for and find the personal in the world about him. It arises in furtherance of poetic and religious sentiments alike. It discloses the spiritual framework of things, and at the same time seeks to adorn it with all the sprightliness of art. It makes the world deeply significant in the only way in which it can at once and equally address the thoughts and the affections. The spiritual and personal are not the yeast of waves that have beaten themselves into foam, the last, slightest, and most solitary of products; they are primordial as well as final, fundamental as well as superficial, that which we are reaching as the deepest, most refreshing truth in all our inquiry. The world is open to art because it is animate; it is religious because it abides everywhere under supersensuous law. The entire search of the truly devout mind is for the personal, the spiritual, the divine in the world; and for the power to abide on terms of sympathy with it. Superstition is the immaturity and distortion of this growth, and yet the religious impulse, in the darkest periods and places, is the one redemptive power, lifting men from an animal basis. Here is a being who can be touched, profoundly touched, by a sense of the invisible; a being who is open to all those motives which come from the spiritual world; a being, therefore, who belongs to that world, and can be brought under its perfect law. This search for the personal, this delight in it, this free subjection in righteousness to it, find full satisfaction only in the supernatural as centred in the Divine Life. So the natural becomes its instant expression. The two elements cease to be estranged from each other, and go forth together as the sensuous and spiritual side of the same movement, a movement always more and greater than its present manifestation. Thus the supernatural loses all waywardness, and the natural all deadness; the two are blended in perfected life.

It is a matter of surprise that the evolutionist passes so lightly the religious tendency in man, a tendency so peculiar, so universal, so controlling, so aspiring. As a simple fact, an actual energy, it deserves far more attention than it receives, implies a far deeper relation than is conceded to it. Instead of being an impulse that can be pushed aside, as a transient, erratic energy, it offers itself as the germ of all upward movement, the one spiritual term which men hold in common. Sensuous motives bring to men no sufficient government. They must be supplemented and replaced by supersensuous ones. The first terms in this advanced and advancing experience have been, and for most men are, contained in the religious life. Errors and failures plead nothing against it. These are a matter of course, and merely mark the steps of development. That faith which most fully contains this personifying tendency, this search of mind for mind, this reproduction of rational life in rational life, shows itself to be a stadium in the upward march, a focus at which all forces are converging.

The natural separated from the supernatural is the slow strangulation of spiritual life. Poetry is a fiction of the feelings, and religion a feebleness of the thoughts; while the world, in all its glorious changes, has no more life or assured promise in it than a top spinning on its axis. Such a conception is too dead to be long entertained even by naturalism, and so there begin to steal in those illogical abatements and insufficient corrections of which this philosophy is so full, and is becoming increasingly full. Life is thought to have a tendency to variation, which can be manipulated by natural selection into something very like progress; and an Unknown is advanced as the ultimate term of thought—an Unknown that can be nursed into a divinity not wholly remote from God. And so the impoverished roots of thought are fed once more by fancy.

It is certainly strange that the ripe reason of the positivist should be employed, in its most extreme and erratic freedom, to set aside the inherent, inevitable movement of reason in the race; and yet the gist of reason remain with the positivist a causal, and not a voluntary, relation. On their own basis, it is absurd for a handful of positivists to flatly contradict the general methods of human thought.

But why should we be content to accept their feeble concessions, to glean these few heads of wheat—often only tares—in a field all our own? If law is that absolute thing with which we start our parable, then all makeshifts in satisfaction of human feeling will turn out illusions. Fate is a mild word for this deadlock of eternity, and human history, with its fears and hopes, and endless shiftiness to the eye, a bitter mockery, when contrasted with its inner, inevitable drift toward the unknown. If this causal law is allowed to break for an instant at a single point, we cannot knit it a second time; we can only regain coherence by passing fully over to that higher unity in spiritual life by which distinct methods are resolved into one movement under the mastery of pure reason.

The second purpose which the supernatural subserves, is that of rest to our higher faculties; and each purpose, let us remember, is an argument in behalf of the supernatural. The only right of being, is a reason for being. This truth is enforced by science. Our empiricism, even, has taught it us all along. We saw many things which we did not understand, that seemed purposeless, or worse than purposeless, in the world. They had the right of being, with no reason for being. This impression, inquiry has steadily dispelled; and we have come to see—not yet completely, but very fully—that a right and a reason have gone together, and things have been chiefly by virtue of the purposes they have subserved. The efficient causes and the final causes have been blended in them as in natural selection. The fittest survive, and they survive because they are the fittest. That which subserves a purpose, that which stands in constructive harmony with other things, for that reason abides in strength. We may figure this relation as an equilibrium of forces, or as an inner coherence of the divine thought. In either way, the right and the reason, the fact and its purpose, go together.

With this second purpose of rest comes the third purpose, which can best be treated with it, of enlargement. We cannot have spiritual rest without spiritual enlargement. Rest is the repose of powers in spiritual activities that sufficiently employ them and reward them. The intellectual constitution makes a demand, quite the equivalent of that of the body, for sufficient air; it refuses to be suffocated; repression is most irksome to it. Range and vitality go together. But there is no enlargement for reason like that which makes reason the universal element in all things. Between this conception and that of universal causal relations there is no comparison in the stimulus offered by them. The one contains the other and much more. Order is admitted by reason up to the line at which it becomes rigid, cold, and dead; at which it ceases to be artistic and spiritual. The supernatural, rightly understood, is an inexhaustible wealth that lies beyond the natural, a light that percolates through the cloud and glorifies it, without dispersing it; that discloses its outlines in changeable interplay with the very element that is streaming through it.

There are peculiarly gifted and noble natures, minds whose intellectuality is of a remarkable order, that find satisfaction in naturalism alone—men like Darwin, whose activity in one direction is so great, so fascinating, so successful, that it swallows up all impulses and fills the entire circle of the powers. But these persons are altogether exceptional; exceptional as men of ability, and exceptional among men of ability. They are not more numerous than are Stoics in society. The stoical attitude is genuine and one of much nobility. It owes this nobility to an exaggeration of the very principle we are enforcing—the power of mind. The Stoic, in asserting this power, finds an exhilaration which he can, in some measure, mistake for satisfaction. But the rest of Stoicism, in a stern defiance of fortune, is very different from that insight which sees fortune forever resolving itself along lines of light into divine favor. The devotee of naturalism, in the enthusiasm of a study of nature, so magnifies intellect, on its practical side, that he overlooks the indignity and weakness he has put upon it theoretically. This quiet of naturalism, pursuing for a brief period the paths of inquiry, is much inferior to that loving faith which makes the spirit forever a denizen of a universe of ideas and ideal affections.

This rest and this enlargement in reason mean everything for the most spiritual minds, and mean very much for the average mind. The impersonal is altogether too cold and abstract for household warmth, for daily affections. The masses of men, if they are to be impelled forward, must find their impulse in things that lie near them, in a love that begets love, in a righteousness that carries its rewards and retributions with it, and, standing at the very portal of the heart, administers them as immediate affections and passions.

It is not the progress of a few, nor the convictions of a few, that are to measure human development, nor to furnish within themselves the conditions of growth for any considerable number in any given period. The leaders of Israel will linger in the wilderness as long as Israel is there. The real question we have always to propound is not, what motives suffice in single minds for brief moments, but what motives are sufficient for all men in the entire stage of growth. Facts answer this question much more exactly than theories. Evidently nothing can be so universally efficient as the expansion of the affections common to us all toward God, and their return thence to a more quiet and pervasive action among ourselves. The love of man is a corollary of the love of God, an item under it; and the love of God keeps pace with our love of men, is an aggregate of it. To expand the affections outward and upward, is to make them restful on their own centre of human love, is to justify universal harmony to the thoughts and to develop it in the feelings at one and the same time, by one and the same process. Rebel against it as we please, the mind can attain to no perfect ideal which is not then and there colored and made vital by the feelings; and the feelings of men are not detached and personal possessions, but part and portion of universal humanity. The daylight that cheers my room receives its quantity and quality from universal light. The universe is made a universe to man's spiritual nature, and filled from bound to bound with its own light by virtue of the love of God, by virtue of the spiritual presence which pervades it. Christ, in revealing this love, in a very direct sense in reflecting it, became the light of the world. He who walks without love, walks in darkness; and love in its supreme form can only belong to a Supernatural Personal Presence. All love must be secondary, derived and trifling compared with this love.

The reasons which lead us to enforce the supernatural are at one with those which urge us to insist on the natural. The supernatural nourishes that sense of power to which the natural gives adequate expression. The two are the equilibrium of strength. Lacking sufficient faith in the natural, we miss the means of wise and successful work. Lacking faith in the supernatural, we fail of the full inspiration and reward of that work. In short periods and with single persons faults of methods will be obscure and partial; for we are living in an atmosphere prepared for us, not in one created by us. Our work, if it has the least depth, must pass on to the next generation for its disclosure. In our efforts to escape the partial forms of faith, we easily slip beyond the lines of growth. We do well to remember that every position in progress, well taken, springs directly from previous ones. The supernatural has wrought in the world's history as a supreme force. The next phase of thought is not its exclusion, but its coalescence with the natural. Those rare manifestations of the supernatural which have given so much offence to the critical temper will then be lost in the pervasive presence of Creative Power. The vitality of the world will not be established by brilliant exceptions, but by habitual on-goings. That the supernatural in the past has by a little overlapped the natural in striking manifestations is quite in keeping with that universal push of life, not yet dominant, by which, within the limits of nature, it has enlarged nature itself. Our very evolution becomes blind and aimless if we undertake to dispense with the supernatural.

CHAPTER III.

DOGMATISM.

DOGMA has played a very extended, and, at times, a very unfortunate, part in Church history. Reformed churches not less than those waiting reform, Protestants even more than Catholics, have attached an importance to doctrines quite beyond the part they are fitted to play in a healthy spiritual life.

Dogma grows up, in the first instance, in satisfaction of the mind. It is the result of an intellectual impulse, and performs, therefore, a service both legitimate and valuable. It is a movement in every way, at its inception, in keeping with the progress of truth. Proportion and balance men always find most difficult to achieve. Not only does each effort tend to excess in itself, later, it is the occasion of a kindred excess in an opposite direction. Hence men are now speaking contemptuously of the speculative tendency of thought, as contrasted with inquiry. As a matter of fact, each is equally essential, and the two supplement each other. Inquiry will reach no goal without the theoretical tendency, and this tendency will exhaust itself in abstractions unless given fresh, fruitful data by inquiry.

The process of deductive thought, which finds expression in dogma, is valid and primary. In mathematics, the results of pure thought are of extended, and of complete, utility. Reasoning, in this direction, is so safe and productive because of the entire simplicity and adequacy of the notions with which it sets out. Speculation so often miscarries in the wider world of facts and events because its primary conceptions are inadequate or untrue. In these directions empirical inquiry must enter the more constantly to enlarge and correct its premises. Hence knowledge, in the physical and moral world, where the data are complex, obscure and changeable, must be won equally by insight and observation, by exposition and an ever renewed search into the facts to be expounded.

Theology has grown almost exclusively by a deductive process. A few root ideas have given form to its conclusions. It has thus, while in itself a most legitimate and desirable attainment, fallen into a double error. It has allowed deduction to push aside induction, while dealing not with simple, abstract ideas, but with most complex and obscure facts; and, from a practical point of view, a still more fatal mistake, it has allowed the speculative interest of thought to take, in part, the place of interest in virtue, in a life thoroughly harmonized within and without with existing conditions of conduct. Thus there has been not only an unwarrantable separation of the two terms in the double processes of acquiring knowledge; there has been a kindred partition of the triple process of conduct.

Thinking has been partially separated from its immediate union with feeling and action, and that in a direction in which all three are most closely affiliated. Speculation has thus ceased to be sound thinking and productive thinking. It has failed from one and the same cause on the theoretical and on the practical side. Its root ideas have not found correction and enlargement in the facts which came under them, and the fresh fruits of conduct and character have been much dwarfed and diminished in amount. The speculative religious life has tended to lose connection with actual life, both in its comprehension and in its government.

It is not strange, under these circumstances, that the pursuit of dogma should have shown a temerity on the one side, and an audacity on the other, equally foreign to its proper intellectual and spiritual temper. Robustness and good-will were both lost. Perhaps no theological discussion ever exhibited this tendency in a more repulsive form than that which attended in the fourth century—a leading century in religious dogma—on the development of the doctrine of the Trinity. Slight, well-nigh unintelligible, and more or less fantastic, distinctions were urged with a vehemence and virulence that broke asunder all the ordinary ties of good-will. The vineyard of God was furiously trampled under foot by the blind rage of those to whom it had been committed.

We would not, for an instant or in any degree, lose sight of the wholly legitimate and very desirable character of a systematic pursuit of Christian doctrine. Both the terms of thought and the terms of action will be much modified by it. It is the result of our general desire of knowledge and safe guidance directed to the very highest field of investigation. We wish, however, to insist that Christian doctrine, as it has to do not with simple, primary conceptions, but with most complex and abstruse ideas, and with an extended survey of the facts included under them, must prosper, as a department of knowledge, not by deduction alone, but by deduction constantly sustained by induction. The speculative methods of theology are neither practically safe nor theoretically justified when we consider the real service that falls to it.

Its field of thought is the moral world—that is, the entire world, looked at in its spiritual relations. No matter whether the growth of knowledge, by which we come increasingly to understand the world as the arena of spiritual life, comes to us by Revelation or by rational inquiry, as knowledge, it must, in the end, distinctly and correctly cover these facts, the moral character of God, the moral discipline of the world, the moral development of man individually and in society. Hence there is no department of thought which addresses itself more directly and comprehensively to facts, near and remote, plain and obscure, than this very inquiry of theology. And hence, again, there is no form of inquiry which should bind together more carefully and cautiously the two processes of mind which we express as deduction and induction.

However we may conceive the character of God, that conception, whether gathered from the Word of God or from various thoughts concerning him, must conform to that presentation of his being which finds expression in his works. This is the truly authoritative declaration, because it is the actual one, and also the very one which Revelation and human thought are present to expound. Our inquiries, therefore, into the nature of God, while resting on the conceptions of good men concerning him, must be accompanied by a constant effort to make our thought of him harmonious and adequate within itself, and by a desire assiduously to correct and enlarge all impressions by putting them into more complete conformity with what the world offers us in a positive and concrete form on the same theme.

The divine nature and the divine character, which constitute fundamental conceptions in theology, are facts which are delineated in another way in the nature and progress of the world about us. Revelation can only make this their immediate relation more clear and explicit. While Revelation interprets the world, the world equally, in turn, interprets Revelation. The light of religious truth is only satisfactory when it brings disclosure to things, and finds full reflection in them. Light is revelation because all objects rejoice in it, and instantly take on, by means of it, their own proper form and beauty. That which waits to be illuminated and habilitated by the Revelation of God are the works of God.

The government of God flows directly from his character; and certainly we cannot study that government, nor accept any presentation of it except in connection with an inquiry into a history of the world and human history, the only products of that government known to us. The obscurity which rests on individual, national, and race development, on the forces which initiate and sustain growth in society and the ends reached by it, is that which drives us to inquiry. This obscurity can only give way before a presentation of the divine method which carries light and guidance into all the affairs of men. We understand the divine mind in and by these affairs.

The nature of man, the nature of sin, the lines and methods of redemption, the spiritual history of the human race, are all themes which teach facts, far and near, and can only be discussed successfully by theology in connection with these facts. However absolute we may suppose Revelation to be, it is not thereby relieved of the necessity of conforming to the facts of which it is treating. We are entitled to an anthropology, a psychology, a sociology, a philosophy of development, and all these forms of knowledge must give us data and principles covering at least a portion of the field of theology. The true sources of truth must conform to each other in their results, or our knowledge falls into hopeless confusion. What we find the nature of man, that Revelation must declare it to be; and what Revelation declares it, that we must find it to be. The two sets of conceptions teach the same facts, and must be brought into harmony by them. Nothing can put down the facts, be it theory or Revelation.

The moral forces which rule the world are the forces which religious truth and social science are both dealing with. The two—social science and theology—have precisely the same problem, expressed on this side as the perfection of society, and on that side as the Kingdom of Heaven. Not only must there be a mutual understanding between these two forms of effort, there must be an extended, yes, a complete interlock of labor; and a theology which seeks the regeneration of society in ignorance of social laws is doomed to failure, and a sociology which does not place prominent among the spiritual powers, the power of faith, is striving to guide men and lead them into excellence without imparting the true life-giving impulse.

The great danger of theology has been, and still is, that it desires to become the finished product of a narrowly deductive process, that it ascribes to its immediate conclusions a divine authority, and thus, in the temper of dogmatism, anticipates all the instruction of scientific inquiry, human history, and God's daily providence; and struggles hard to put upon the growing products of thought, as fast as they arise, a narrow construction of its own. The deductive tendency naturally runs in advance of the inductive, and often submits with an ill grace to its ally when it arrives. Yet, if the divine mind and method are to be pre-eminently associated with either of these two forms of thought, they are to be united to the inductive, rather than to the deductive, process, to the child-like temper rather than to the philosophic temper, to the grand procession of events in which the thoughts of God are unfolding themselves rather than to our curious speculations concerning them, or expansion of the earlier forms of our thought about them. The Messiah never meets the expectations of those who are waiting for him. It is the mind that must ever submit itself to the divine ordination of events.

A kindred difficulty has shown itself even in science. Those who, in youth, have made great additions to knowledge, and brought to it the light of new principles, are frequently, in old age, disposed to restrain the very methods of inquiry by which they have prospered, simply because these methods are tending to bring further and unacceptable modifications of opinion. But this slight inflexibility in scientific thought, troublesome as it sometimes is, is nothing to the inflexibility of theological conclusions, wedded to their lines of deductive reasoning, and filled with a sense of divine revelation. The proper relation of religious truth to practical experience is, in itself, so important, and a recognition of it is so necessary to any right understanding of theology, that we shall be pardoned if we present it somewhat fully.

Let us take such a system of religious faith as that offered by Dr. Charles Hodge, in his "Systematic Theology." This voluminous treatise may well enough stand for other systems, because it is a recent one, and one not very extreme in its conclusions nor unusual in its methods. He starts with the assertion that the Scriptures contain all the facts of theology. "Theology is the exhibition of the facts of Scripture, in their proper order and relation, with the principle or general truths involved in the facts themselves." The theology which follows, however, is almost exclusively a discussion of the principles thought to be contained in the facts and teachings of Scripture, and far more in its teachings than in its facts. Its facts, as facts simply, are placed at their lowest value. The force and pith of them are found in the words which accompany them. Inspiration is held to give exact truth, and this belief lifts the burden of inquiry from the circumstances which accompany the words of the sacred writer, and directs it to the words themselves. Indeed, under this view of the nature of Revelation, facts lose most of their significance. They are only the framework of the picture. They may enhance its impression, but do not determine its nature. They are occasions, but not controlling causes. The truth has its inner perfection aside from those to whom, and by whom, it was spoken. If facts are to be treated as facts, they must be allowed their full efficiency, and a careful, historic inquiry must unfold the growth of truth under them and by them. If the development of the truth is relatively independent of them, by being of a divine order, most of the value of the facts as interpreting terms is taken from them. Mathematical truth is not dependent for its force on occasions; in an important sense it has no occasions, as it is absolute within itself and unaffected by any particular application. This system, like most systems, is not exegetical in a historic way, but regards the declarations of Scripture, at all periods by all persons, as final, and simply sets itself the task of a systematic statement of the truths they are supposed to contain. Supernatural facts, indeed, receive some attention; but merely natural facts trail on in the shadow of the ruling, divine manifestation that is always rising above them. Hardly any inquiry, therefore, is more thoroughly deductive, under the lead of a few initiative ideas, than the investigation which issues in this "Systematic Theology." While no objection is taken to the method simply because it is deductive, the fact calls for the utmost caution in attaining the data from which the deduction is to proceed, and in establishing the tests and the independent sources of correction by which it is to be sustained and restrained at every stage of progress.

The principles which make up systematic theology are not pure, mental conceptions. They are ideas which owe their entire value to their perfect correspondence with obscure and complex facts. They involve the relations which lie between these facts in their final interpretation. The definition we may frame of God must find its correctness not merely in its logical coherence, but in its power to express to us the origin and growth of the universe. Our doctrine of the atonement must correspond with the moral incentives we experience day by day, and disclose their vital power.

This system of theology, in common with many another, makes little provision for correct data, or for testing the conclusions that are arising under them. These data include two terms—the accepted powers of mind and the specific affirmations of the text. The powers of mind may be inferred from the text, or the text, in its meaning, may be shaped to meet an antecedent conception of the powers of mind. That is to say, we may derive our philosophy from our theology, or we may reach our theology through our philosophy. The reverent mind, which insists on the absolute character of Revelation, naturally inclines to the first method. The second set of data, the inspired teachings, are regarded as complete in themselves, and carry with them, by easy inference, the prior data. All things, therefore, are now ready, and every truth can be wrung from the text. No assumption could more simplify the process of deduction and divest it of all preliminary difficulties. The supposition of complete inspiration greatly reduces also the need of verification in the progress of the deductive process. Deduction, if you have absolute premises, is one of the clearest and safest movements of mind. This fact systematic theology is sure to remember, and it comes, therefore, with its final results, fully prepared to overbear any facts which may stand in their way. Far from correcting its interpretation by the facts, it corrects the facts by its divinely certain rendering of them. The facts are bidden, with no gentle voice, to stand one side. Nothing but the plainest contradiction disturbs the dogmatic temper, and even this contradiction it denies so long as it is possible to do so. Thus such questions as the creation of the world, the origin of man, the time of his appearance on the earth, his primitive state, the form of his historic development, are first pronounced upon, then discussed wholly upon the defensive, and made to suffer in their consideration all the distortion of an inflexible theory, a theory whose inflexibility is kept constantly at a maximum, being that of revealed truth. Thus the worst dangers of deduction are made unavoidable and are perpetually recurrent.

If we were to allow the legitimacy of deduction so employed,—which we certainly cannot—it still remains true that we do not secure the footing by means of it we are thought to attain. Take the most fundamental doctrine of all, the nature of God. Dr. Hodge regards—and it may well be so regarded—the definition of the Westminster Catechism as among the most complete—" God is a spirit, infinite, eternal, and unchangeable in his being, wisdom, power, holiness, justice, goodness, and truth." How is a definition of this kind framed?

It is shaped under our growing conception of the harmony of attributes in a perfect being. We cannot put it together mechanically, bit by bit, its several parts being taken from the Bible. We may immensely quicken the mind in framing it by a study of the spirit and power of the Scriptures, but the definition remains ours, remains that of the Westminster Catechism, and not that of the Bible. The whole formative process is one of utmost delicacy and insight, and must turn, in its fulness and correctness, on the intellectual development and spiritual penetration of those who are at work on it. Many statements of Scripture must receive fitting abatement in its formation. The anger, jealousy, and repentance of God, and his propitiation by us, must take a meaning in harmony with the conception, and must not themselves be allowed to color it. That is to say, the process of inclusion and rejection, of increase and diminution, must proceed under the rational activity of the constructive mind, directed toward the Scriptures, toward human history, and toward all ultimate truths. This fundamental statement in all theology, the nature of God, is not a pure, unmistakable product of Revelation, but one to be attained in connection with it, with varying success, according to the insight and temper brought to the undertaking. We owe this particular definition to the Westminster Divines. They are the lens of this light, the immediate medium between us and God. Their perspicuity is our insight.

Pass this point. Take the definition just as it is; allow

it the authority of Scripture, and yet it is no safe datum for heroic deduction. It is not a definition—very far from it—whose meaning is precise and unmistakable. The words point out directions of thought rather than lay down its limits. Here is a fundamental difficulty with the authority assigned such dogmas. The Scriptures are not philosophical in phraseology, nor would the matter be much helped if they were. They give no definitions to their words; these words search our own experience for explanation. Their meaning will be as full and correct as our thinking can make it, no more so. This is a fact fatal to absolute truth, when the conceptions are complex; and to the use of Biblical assertions as the unilluminated premises of final conclusions. Words are the counters of thought, and the word, in our use of it, can be no more exact than is the thinking in which it takes part.

Return to the definition. What do we understand by the words, spirit, infinite, eternal?

It may be the slightness, rather than the exactness, of our apprehension of these words that causes us to be so content with our comprehension of them. Many thoughtful minds are very much baffled by them, and systems of philosophy turn on the intelligibility or unintelligibility of these ideas. This fact is no serious difficulty so far as the wholesome, nutritive processes of each mind are concerned, but is entirely fatal, if we undertake to reach results authoritative for all minds.

When we pass on to those other words, "unchangeable in his being, wisdom, power, holiness, justice, goodness, and truth," we are dealing with conceptions so rich and comprehensive that while we grasp much we miss far more. They are most unfit words on which to fasten a deductive process in an exhaustive way. Who but the perfectly wise can tell what wisdom involves; who but the completely good can lay down the laws of goodness? We might as well attempt to infer the next phase of a sunset from the one now before us, as the succeeding methods of God from previous ones. In each case, in spite of all causal connections, we must sit quietly by and see the vision unfold itself in its own inexhaustible glories.

In what sense is God unchangeable? If we were to say that he is infinitely flexible, we should have uttered a truth of equal scope.

What is meant by the unchangeableness of the divine character can only be understood by seeing how far steadfastness is an element of perfection; and this we must learn from a growing knowledge of the physical and spiritual conditions of our being. It need not be urged further that we have no definitions of holiness, justice, goodness, truth, other than those which our own experience supplies, and that it is the ever ripening fruit of that experience to impart to these words a deeper and more purified significance. There can be, then, in our knowledge of God's moral attributes—the most essential form of religious truth—nothing more final and profound than our present experiences of moral qualities can furnish. We readily recognize the difficulty of imparting just conceptions of God to a barbarous people. The embarrassment is the same in kind when the most cultivated races and persons approach these ultimate problems of life, these transcendent truths of being. We should see little significance in immortality, if we had already penetrated the revelation of God to its very core. Theology, because its fundamental ideas are so profound, finds in them no fitting premises for a reasoning that is to reach at once finalities.

This is already seen in such a doctrine as that of the Trinity. The most explicit statements are the most inadequate, and are hardly intelligible, not to say convincing. The Scriptural data on which the doctrine rests are exceedingly loose and figurative, and give no premises to exact statement. They cannot be subjected to the pressure of a logical process without yielding absurdity on this side and illusion on that. One must be left to make such uses of an article of faith of this order as his own thoughts call for. To break in analysis through its dramatic, representative imagery is to incur the utmost risk of folly, and is to carry with us no authority whatever.

No better example in the "Systematic Theology" referred to of unsafe deduction can be found than that offered by the doctrines of regeneration, justification, and sanctification. Regeneration is virtually re-creation by the Divine Spirit. Justification is a forensic—forensic!—act made possible by imparting to us the righteousness of Christ; and sanctification is due to the power of God over and above the power of the second causes concerned. Conclusions like these are derived from each other, and rest on a special philosophy of human powers. If that philosophy is correct they may be correct; if it is untrue, they cannot stand. If the acts of a free agent are fully embraced in the decrees of God, as Dr. Hodge thinks, then what we call freedom, responsibility, guilt, virtue, are very different things from the conceptions we cover by these words, if we believe that the human mind has the power to choose between good and evil, and that the problem of a moral life is wrought out at this very point of choice. We are not discussing the correctness of the two views; we are only insisting that each of them must turn, in its authority, on a sound philosophy of human life. No theologian, in these and kindred doctrines, can escape the quagmire which surrounds this question of freedom. He must plunge in with the rest of us, and make what strides and strokes he can for the farther shore. Scripture does not help him over this obstacle. Its language is popular, and, like popular language, waits for philosophical interpretation. In arguing for freedom we should certainly urge the considerations that this belief gives a much more adequate meaning to language, is a better expression of the popular thought, and corresponds more directly with the commands and exhortations of Scripture. We certainly should not say that we were entitled to an affirmative conclusion on the ground of the injunctions of the Bible. We should recognize the fact that these words, and all words, remain to be interpreted by the very relations which they cover, and that we are not safe in our conclusions till the two are brought together. Certainly, then, we can concede no authority whatever to the verbal inferences of Dr. Hodge beyond that which attaches to the philosophy which sustains them. It is a grave abuse of inspiration, even if we believe it to cover the very words of the text, to affirm that it precludes our interpretation of the text. This, at least, remains, and must stand or fall by its own wisdom.

The "Systematic Theology" sustains its dogma of sanctification by such passages as these: "And the very God of peace sanctify you wholly."[1] "Now the God of peace, that brought again from the dead our Lord Jesus, that great Shepherd of the sheep, through the blood of the everlasting covenant, make you perfect in every good work, to do his will, working in you that which is well pleasing in his sight, through Jesus Christ."[2] Words like

[1] 1 Thess. v., 23. [2] Heb. xiii., 20, 21.

these are to be rendered, and can only be rendered, in the light of our own experience. We are to improve this rendering by getting nearer and yet nearer to the very facts of life, and the method of God in them. This is the divine discipline of living, and a discipline often grievously interrupted by theology. Its predetermined temper reads into profound words like these, a narrow rendering which is termed systematic merely because it has forced the meaning into a logical form far too strait for it.

The dogma of justification, as a forensic act, springs out of the dogma of a supernatural regeneration, and from the two arises the dogma of an atonement, in which the sufferings and righteousness of Christ take the place of our own righteousness and sufferings. Thus we build up a theological block-house in defiance of ethical principles, and we pass righteousness backward and forward as if it were a commodity of the market. Ethics insists on regeneration as a correction of the soul within the soul itself. If it is not so purified it remains unregenerate. The moral law pushes its way into the soul of man as the form and force of its life. To have moral life is to have it, is to enter by clear consciousness and well ordered obedience into truth. Strangely enough, under this systematic view, sin and righteousness can be imputed, and when so imputed they are just as potent as when real. The forensic penalty cannot be overcome by forgiveness. That is, the purely formal element is more unchangeable than the substantial element. Sin can be gotten rid of by imputation, but being imputed cannot be escaped without punishment. Ethics, in the face of all these cunning ways, affirms the inherent character of moral action; that sin and righteousness are states inseparable from the conduct in which they inhere, and thus the consequences of action follow on the actions themselves. Forgiveness turns on repentance, and is until seventy times seven. Why? because true repentance begets a new life.

Our purpose, however, is not to argue these points. What we wish to affirm is that they are one and all open to argument, that the conclusions we reach are no sounder than the premises on which they rest, and that the truth is found by an explanatory process which unites the entire work and the entire word of God. Whether guilt demands a punishment definite in amount and in no way to be avoided; whether this penalty can be transferred; what are the fruits of repentance; these and kindred inquiries are to be answered by a right rendering of human history as well as inspired thought. The "Systematic Theology" is in no way entitled, as a sound deduction from undeniable premises, to the certainty of any of its conclusions. An implication of this order is simply the lack of intelligence or of fairness.

Dr. Hodge, in defence of his doctrine of justification, gives a few passages of Scripture, which hardly bear on the subject otherwise than verbally: "I will not justify the wicked,"[1] "Wisdom is justified of her children."[2] "But he, willing to justify himself, said unto Jesus, And who is my neighbor?"[3] He then proceeds to put himself under the shelter of St. Paul: "Knowing that a man is not justified by the works of the law, but by the faith of Jesus Christ, even we have believed in Jesus Christ, that we might be justified by the faith of Christ, and not by the works of the law; for by the works of the law shall no flesh be justified."[4] "For in Christ Jesus neither

---

[1] Ex. xxiii., 7. [2] Matt. xvi., 19.
[3] Luke x., 29. [4] Gal. ii., 16.

circumcision availeth anything, nor uncircumcision; but faith, which worketh by love."[1] "Even as David also describeth the blessedness of the man unto whom God imputeth righteousness without works."[2]

St. Paul is the favorite apostle of the theologian. Probably more extreme dogmas have been extracted from the epistles of St. Paul than from all the Bible besides. They readily lend themselves to this use, or, as it may quite as fittingly be termed, this abuse. A logical precision is referred to these epistles which is very foreign to them, while the exact conditions under which they were written, and the immediate purposes they were intended to subserve, are largely overlooked. The justness of the precise criticism we are now enforcing, a neglect of facts in the making up of dogma, is very conspicuous in the manner in which the words of St. Paul are employed.

In the wide, changeable field of religious truth, those principles will receive especial emphasis at any one time by any one writer which have gotten peculiar force in his own thoughts, and in the demands of his own experience. They are necessarily, therefore, for the moment thrown out of proportion with other principles, and may seem to assume a character more fundamental than really belongs to them. Even when the discussion itself does not exaggerate them, the very fact of the discussion causes them to fill the eye, to the exclusion of other things. This partial and disproportionate presentation of truth pervades human thought; and when it appears in the writings of an apostle, it becomes more than usually mischievous, because of the assumption of the completeness and symmetry of the Scriptures. Two things are overlooked in the use of the writings of St. Paul which can

[1] Gal. v., 6. [2] Rom. iv., 6.

never be safely neglected—the force of individual tendencies in the writer and the force of historic circumstances. These two things give us the proper background for the apprehension of the words of any man. If they are forgotten, and, like an ambient mist, allowed to mingle with the very things affirmed, they are sure to disguise and distort the truths involved. This transient force of principles, due to powerful prevalent conditions, is seen in the epistles of St. Paul, especially in the epistles to the Romans and to the Galatians. The very form and purpose of an epistle tend to give it local, personal coloring, and to separate it widely from a systematic statement of truth. A doctrine of inspiration which attaches slight weight to the naturalism of times, persons, and purposes, exposes the theologian to great danger. This fact is clearly illustrated in the uses which have been made of the writings of St. Paul. They have been treated as if they were a collection of aphorisms, each seen in its own light, and not a glowing discussion of urgent practical problems of somewhat narrow compass. The local elements are not allowed their true weight. The human conditions are permitted to color the divine message, greatly to its limitation. Few inspired writers are more stimulating than St. Paul, if we share his freedom and force of movement. For this very reason his words are least of all fit to be taken in a detached way and reduced into dogma by forceful deduction.

St. Paul was a man of intense temper. His entire experience confirmed this ardor of conviction. He did not take religious truth lightly, nor urge it in a reserved manner. Before his conversion, and after it, his opinions pressed his own mind and brought corresponding pressure to the minds of other men. He was an apostle of the truth, in a pre-eminent sense—warm in feeling, aggressive in thought, bold in action. Whatever phase his life assumed, it assumed with an energy that paid little heed to reservations and proportions. His description of himself is, "As touching the law, a Pharisee; concerning zeal, persecuting the church; touching the righteousness which was in the law, blameless."[1]

The circumstances of the life of St. Paul were such as to give the fullest expression to this ardent, spiritual habit of mind, and to involve him deeply and constantly in the most circumscribed and bitter religious controversy of his time, the relation of the Jewish law to the law of Christ, the liberty of every man with the truth. His own early method of thought and connection with the Jewish leaders, and his later position as the apostle of the Gentiles, forced him into the heat of this discussion, and compelled him to bear, both on its theoretical and practical side, the brunt of the conflict. There thus fell to his lot the most intense personal obloquy and hostility.

The law stood with the Jews and with St. Paul, not for ethical law, as we understand it, but for a very complex, extended, and vexatious set of commands, that penetrated into the entire life of a devotee, and took complete possession of religious action, to the exclusion of anything like insight and personal liberty. A free, vigorous mind must fully adopt such a system, or find itself in irreconcilable hostility to it. Whatever concessions St. Paul might have been willing, personally, to make to this Jewish ritual of life, as a preacher of the Gospel to the Gentiles, he was compelled to antagonize it. The universal nurture of grace must not be destroyed

[1] Philip. iii., 5, 6.

by the nurture of a worn-out national faith. If the Gentile, in his discipleship, had been compelled to accept the Jewish law, not only would it have laid on him a burden impossible to be borne, the very effort to bear it would at once have obscured the gift of grace, and closed to the vision of the mind the true path of life. Such had been its effect, in a large measure, on the Jews themselves, though the law stood to them, by virtue of their history, in a relation it could never sustain to another people. It fell to St. Paul to discuss and re-discuss the bearings of the Jewish law on the grace of Christ, and to resist the insidious efforts to straiten the divine method by the devices of men. This controversy involved the general question, which has arisen so often and in so many forms, —the connection of the inner life with the acts which express it.

This discussion has widened in religious history into an effort to define the relation of faith and works, and has owed its extreme position, its obscurity, obstinacy, and gross errors, not to its inherent difficulty, but to the want of spirituality in men. A very little insight carries the mind to a position from which any conflict between faith and works wholly disappears. The warmth of daylight dispels the mist at once. Works are the inevitable expression of faith, and faith is the living force of works. A fact which has helped to keep this controversy alive, and added so much to its confusion, has been the mingling in it of the moral and the ritual elements of law. These two terms stand, in any system which embraces them both, in very different relations to conduct and religious nurture. The Jewish law not only embraced them both, it overshadowed them both with endless traditions, which attached the utmost importance to multiplied forms of action, aside from the spirit which animated them. Thus an authority was attributed to the tradition which belonged only to the ritual, and to the ritual which properly attached only to the moral command. Confusion of thought prevailed everywhere. The least and the largest injunctions were made to rest on the same authority, and an act which subserved no purpose of nurture was regarded as binding as an ethical precept. The conventional minds of men have again and again fallen into a hopeless quagmire in considering the primitive laws of God, and their own foolish extensions of them. They have failed to vindicate the freedom of each mind with the truth. In fact the freedom of the individual has not been possible to him, embraced as he has been in a community, groping its obscure way in the most intense darkness. Men have been compelled to take each other by the hand, and stumble on as best they could together. The purely moral element of the Jewish law, by its association with rites and traditions, lost very largely its moral quality, and became acts to be rendered in external obedience rather than with inner affections. The law was thus a worthless body bereft of the inner spirit of life.

All that St. Paul has to say about the law, and the works of the law, as contrasted with faith in Christ and the grace of Christ, should be interpreted in view of this accumulated blight of national bigotry, and the complete confusion into which the Jewish mind had fallen as to the law in its triple elements—eternal principle, disciplinary rite, and worthless tradition. The law was treated as a whole by the apostle in the manner in which it was regarded by the Jews, and so condemned in the form and temper of its use. The salient feature of that use was observance divorced from love.

If, however, we read the epistle to the Romans with that insight which should belong to us, taught by the history of two thousand years; if we make the epistle thoroughly consistent with itself by subordinating it to its primary purpose, we shall have no difficulty in seeing that faith with the apostle means the inner hold of the mind on spiritual truth; that works, as opposed to it, stand for formal obedience to the Jewish law; and that redemption, righteousness, justification, are all spiritual states, and not forensic relations. Indeed, the forensic temper was the very thing with which the whole epistle was at strife. If Paul had recognized the work of Christ as another expression of this formal method, he would have been at bottom concurrent with the Jewish feeling. What he was struggling for was the freedom of the soul with truth, with Christ, and with God. Whatever assertions obscure this fact arose from the great darkness which had fallen on the field of human conduct, a darkness which could not be lifted at once and equally in all directions. The light was caught by snatches, and came streaming in by floods, but had not become a mild, universal presence. Paul was simply pressing forward toward the mark of his high calling.

The life-long conflict which St. Paul found occasion to wage with the narrow methods of Judaism and blind belief in favoritism in divine things finds freest and most extended expression in the epistle to the Romans. This epistle, if interpreted from the midstream of the apostolic feeling, is not difficult of apprehension. If it is approached with a subtile, rather than with a profound, spirit, as something to be verbally weighed out for the dialectic process to compound, we shall meet with much confusion and darkness and extreme doctrine.

The apostle first insists that all men have a measure of spiritual life, and so find the conditions of obedience and disobedience. He then affirms that all men are judged by the manner in which they respond to these motives. The advantage of the Jew lies in a larger revelation of the divine mind. But no man has been faithful to the truth.

All have sinned and come short of the glory of God. All, therefore, Jew and Gentile, call for the discipline of Christ, the discipline of forgiveness and love. The point is then made, which is the essential truth of the discussion, that redemption is inward grace and not a product of obedience under the law. It is here that confusion of thought so easily enters. The works of the law are to be interpreted as the complex, burdensome, and artificial impositions of the Jewish service, rendered in a perfunctory way, and not as a loving recognition of the will of God in our own moral constitution. The moral element, so far as it enters into this obedience, enters on the formal side, and is swallowed up in a cumbersome system of observances. That it is the Jewish law, in its mixed elements and punctilious exactions, that was in the mind of the apostle, is seen in the words, "Behold, thou art called a Jew, and restest in the law.[1]"

The contrast which the apostle institutes, and which was made plain by the gross facts with which he was dealing, was precisely this between the spirit of trust, issuing in real obedience to God, and a formal observance of certain commands that carried with it no love of righteousness. The justification of which the apostle speaks is grace hidden in the heart, is a renewal of the

[1] Rom. ii., 17.

entire temper, and not a formal relation to God. There is in the discussion not the least separation between spirit and conduct,—it was this very separation on the part of the Jews that occasioned the controversy—but the affirmation rather that the spirit carries the conduct with it. If we try to secure conduct independently of the temper of trust, conduct becomes dead, and we are swept in under a universal condemnation. If we accept the true dependence of outward life on inward faith, we establish both. Abraham was not justified by works, technical obedience, because his acceptance preceded the law under which the observance arose. It was a living trust in God which gave him divine favor. So we have access by faith into his grace, wherein we stand, and rejoice in the hope of God.

The apostle, in the fifth chapter, dwells on the love of Christ, and the sweep of its power. That this movement of the soul upward in the love of Christ is to be interpreted in a spiritual way, and not in forensic fashion, is abundantly shown by explicit declarations and by the entire force of the argument. Sin came by the contagion of sin; disobedience followed as the entail of disobedience. So righteousness comes as the fruit of righteousness, and love follows the free gift of love. The whole argument is a struggle with a formal, mechanical way of looking at things, a method that puts acts in the place of the feelings that vitalize them, and exterior and national relations for interior and personal ones. We cannot, therefore, admit that justification with the apostle stands for a judicial act without restoring to the heart of the discussion that very thing which it was designed to expel. Understand the words spiritually, and the argument holds throughout: understand them formally, and confusion and contradiction enter everywhere. Justification is a justification of life. It is not, in the attitude implied, to be distinguished from righteousness. God is righteous (just), and the maker righteous (the justifier) of him who believeth in Jesus. To be righteous is to be just, and to be just is to be justified. "The free gift is of many offences unto justification."[1] How can we suppose that the justification here intended is merely formal, and so leaves the inner problem of life to still be resolved?

The following chapter dwells at length on the living character of this redemption. "How shall we, that are dead to sin, live any longer therein?"[2] We are baptized into the death of Christ—his rejection of a sensuous life—that we may walk with him in newness of life. We are dead, indeed, unto sin, but alive unto God, through Jesus Christ our Lord. Being made free from sin and become servants to God, we have fruit unto holiness, and the end everlasting life. The law is thus displaced, in the deadness of its letter, by a life rendered in newness of spirit, and so the righteousness of the law—righteousness sought after by the law—is fulfilled in us, who walk not after the flesh but after the spirit. "To be carnally minded is death, to be spiritually minded is life and peace."[3] "Ye are not in the flesh but in the Spirit, if so be that the Spirit of God dwell in you. Now if any man have not the Spirit of Christ, he is none of his."[4] "As many as are led by the Spirit of God, they are the sons of God."[5] If we allow these words to be, what they seem to be, the inner light of the entire topic, our interpretation becomes convincing and stimulating, and we push our way through the accumulated cobwebs of dogma with a

[1] Rom. v., 16.   [2] Rom. vi., 2.   [3] Rom. viii., 6.
[4] Rom. viii., 9.   [5] Rom. viii., 14.

free, elastic step. We have grasped the fundamental truth which the Jew would not receive—that our relation to God is a personal, spiritual one. Henceforward the confusion about faith and works seems to us one of those blind passages into which men are constantly stumbling as they grope their way upward. The righteousness which is of faith does not ascend into heaven, or descend into hell, in search of Christ or a way of life by him; it finds his word of truth close at hand, in the very heart of the believer. This new feeling of certainty arises from a strictly historical, and a collective, rendering of the epistle.

It is quite true that a more narrow meaning can frequently be read into the words of the apostle, taken as proof-texts; but in the very degree in which this is done, we put ourselves alongside those against whom the epistle was directed. The epistle is a plea for life against a dogma that, in its dry, stiff contraction, was extinguishing life and giving occasion to the spiritual fungi of division, pride, and bitterness. Some passages must be interpreted more narrowly than the first force of the words may seem to allow, in order to bring them into harmony with the epistle as a whole. But this is a result that ought not to disturb us when we are dealing with a mind so fervid, so concentrate in its action, and so little critical, as that of St. Paul. Thus in the ninth chapter, when the apostle is asserting the freedom of God against those who would bind him over under promises to the Jewish nation, his words gather a scope which seems to make the actions of God arbitrary. "O man, who art thou that repliest against God? Shall the thing formed say to him who formed it, Why hast thou made me thus?"[1] This is meeting a factious temper somewhat in

[1] Rom. ix., 20.

its own spirit. But the argument does not call for arbitrary action on the part of God; rather the reverse. If God is arbitrary in his choices, then might he accept the Jew arbitrarily without any change in character; but if he himself is perfectly reasonable, he must look for soundness of life in those who are granted access to him. The example of Jacob and Esau, accepted and rejected antecedently to any manifestation of character, is entirely good for the purpose of showing that the liberty of God is not swallowed up in compacts; but we use it to the subversion of truth when we infer from it unreason in God. We do much better to believe that the apostle was looking at the history narrowly to enforce his own conclusion.

There has been much, too much, weight attached to an alleged discrepancy of opinion and division of policy between St. Paul and St. James. St. James evidently held firmly the very gist of the truth. His statement—Show me thy faith without thy works, and I will show you my faith by my works—touches at once and unerringly the very marrow of the topic. Show me thy health without strength, and I will show you my health by my strength. What more remains to be said? It is only by a misleading side-light that St. Paul is made to attach any other office to faith than this of breathing itself out as life. The entire relation is so simple and unequivocal that it requires some external pressure to pervert it in vision. The two things, faith and the fruits of faith, like the images in the two eyes, will fall together of their own accord, if no violence is used. While we may be surprised at the persevering folly of men in separating them, we may readily see that this division is an illusion of interest or of indolence. The separation is not unlike that between real value and value in use in a currency. The effort to secure a permanent paper value has been a persistent folly in commerce. The formal and the substantial have been found indivisible. Value has slipped from the promise to pay the moment a suspicion of its fulfilment has overtaken it. It is not the images of things, but things themselves, that men wish to deal with, and any want of substance means to them want of reality. We cannot turn works into a sound spiritual currency otherwise than by hiding under them a living faith.

The practical relation of St. James to the Jewish law—which came at once under discussion because of its burdensome formal element—was very different from that of St. Paul, partly because of a difference of character, and partly because of the circumstances under which the two were placed. The very zeal with which St. Paul devoted himself to the law in his earlier life evinced an ardor of temperament that rendered him equally impatient of it when he found it embarrassing the work he had undertaken.

St. James, trained to a quiet observance of its minute regulations, not only suffered little annoyance from them, he doubtless made them terms, artificial as they were, in the expression of a potent and profound religious temper. The law thus fulfilled in him its best possible service. As he confined his labors to the vicinity of Jerusalem, his acceptance of the law aided, rather than hindered, him in his work. He dealt chiefly with those who could make, and were disposed to make, the same use of it as himself, and who found, therefore, no occasion for any violent transition in the forms of piety. Such changes in the outward conditions of life are very trying, and the demand, in connection with them, was exactly reversed with the disciples of St. James and those of St. Paul. The former would seek to be excused from any unnecessary opprobrium by rejecting the religious usages about them, and the latter would as earnestly desire that no unusual and vexatious customs should be imposed upon them. The form, therefore, which identically the same spirit would assume in the two cases would be quite distinct. Faith in Christ would assert, in the one instance, its liberty to obey, and, in the other, its liberty to disobey. Both obedience and disobedience were equally within the scope of religious liberty. When the synod at Jerusalem adjusted the question, it singled out those customs which had a moral force, and enjoined them to the exclusion of all indifferent rules of conduct. They thus put a marked distinction between the ethical command and the traditional custom.

In the case of St. John we have a life which lay somewhat between that of St. Paul and that of St. James. He dealt with both Jews and Gentiles. His own disposition was of that loving, emotional order, which led him to a line of conduct neither intellectually critical, on the one hand, nor narrowly observant of customs, on the other. The words of Christ which he treasures are those addressed to spiritual insight and to the affections; words which call for a close union of the life of the disciple with that of the master. This message of love is on his lips the supreme one. It is a message that admits in conduct no separation between substance and form, and makes light in theory, as it does in practice, of differences in the manner of expressing an overruling sentiment.

Whenever in the history of the Church the religious life has cumbered itself with much serving, a washing of pots and kettles, there has come the occasion for a fresh assertion of the doctrine of faith, and often, unfortunately, for its extreme assertion. Thus when Luther found himself confronted with a traffic in spiritual things, with works of penance and works of merit which were not works of virtue, or works of virtue thrown out of their true relation to morality; when men were losing all spiritual values in a surreptitious currency of empty promises, he met the tendency by a renewed assertion of the fundamental character of faith. In keeping with the division of thought that had already taken place, he took an extreme position, lost sympathy with St. James, perverted St. Paul, and fell into the error of supposing that faith itself might have a formal value aside from the inner and outer changes it works. We rarely correct an error from the midway position of truth, but more often from the extreme position of the opposite error. Thus the error itself often re-introduces itself in its very rectification.

From time to time ritualism seeks to offer a more visible and decisive movement toward a religious life, and men are then restored to personal freedom only by a more positive affirmation of our direct union to God in faith. Hardly anything discloses more completely the ease with which thought becomes superficial and inconsequent than the fact that the re-assertion of faith so often falls into the error it seeks to escape, and makes of itself a definite act with forensic consequences. The truth embarrasses us as much by its simplicity as by its complexity.

The topic now considered, the relation of faith and works, is to be understood, as presented by St. Paul, in connection with the narrow idea of works which held possession of the Jewish mind. The history of the Church for many generations was gathered up in this monstrous perversion, judged from a rational point of view, of the religious life, which St. Paul was called upon to confront. The same question may, indeed, be raised in connection with pure morality, but only as that morality separates itself from its inner life in the affections; or struggles to exclude one injunction by a more exact obedience to another. Works, as faulty, are only the curdling, in one fashion or another, of the milk of human kindness.

The doctrine of the atonement is especially one which should be studied inductively, in a historic spirit. If we look upon the Jewish sacrifices as directly ordered of God for the very purpose of prefiguring the work of Christ, and leading up to it, we shall give a very different place to the sacrificial element in the atonement from that which we shall assign it, if Jewish history rests on natural causes, and is closely interlocked with the general history of the world. We thus regard the sacrifices of the Jewish ritual as due to the same tendencies of thought which gave occasion, in other nations, to similar forms. While the Jews are remarkably distinguished from other peoples by a comparatively free entrance of religious truth through men extraordinarily moved in their own experience by the Divine Spirit, they are closely allied to the nations about them, and to their own period of development, by very limited conceptions of the character of God, and narrow ways of approach to him. Studied historically, sacrifices are at no time a luminous and sufficient form of worship, a just presentation of man's relations to God, but simply one of those early ways of approach which offered themselves to men in their ignorance and their fear. Sacrifices are the natural output of the religious idea working its way upward in darkness and doubt. Ignorance led men to believe that God called for some kind of conciliation, and that a sacrifice might subserve this purpose; and fear prompted them to be very full and circumspect in this method of approach to God. The ritual of the temple service was thus allied to that of many another temple, appealed in the same way to prevalent notions, rooted itself in the same soil of obscure thought, was open to the same abuses, and transcended other forms of discipline chiefly in being accompanied, in the instruction of the prophets, with far more insight and spiritual life.

Sacrifices were capable, with all their misconceptions, of conveying truth; they were a religious training, though an insufficient one. It was their very insufficiency which made the presence and teachings of Christ so needful and so revolutionary. Though God does not call for propitiation, nor need to be turned from his anger by a gift, men do need reconciliation with him. Pressed by this necessity, they inevitably conceive the anger of God as the difficulty to be overcome. God is angry with the wicked every day. They have not reached the spiritual elevation at which they can separate this assertion into its two terms, righteous rejection and personal resentment, see the incompatibility of the two, and at the same time understand that this affirmation of anger, inadmissible in its precise form, stands for the fundamental fact of the moral world. A love that is abhorrent of sin and so compassionate of the sinner, that forces its way between disobedience and the disobedient, that vanquishes transgression by winning the transgressor, is beyond their thought, is too bright a revelation for their steady beholding. This is the revelation in Christ, and the ritual prepared the way for it because it stood for a sincere effort to draw near to God, and because it largely failed of success. It thus pushed men forward to another struggle. Paul thus says of it, that it was a burden that neither we nor our fathers were able to bear; and that it was a servant to lead us to Christ.

If we attach full weight to the historic circumstances which give occasion and coloring to the truth, our interpretation of Scripture will be much modified. We shall not look upon a sacrificial system as enclosing the very work of Christ, but as giving way to it; not as reflecting the truth with precision, but as leading the mind to search for it in a new direction. The transition will be a real transition from a lower to a higher position, from a partial to a corrected conception, from the altar to the foot of the cross, from God to be conciliated to God conciliating all things in his eternal love.

Thus Christ fulfils the law and the prophets in the highest possible sense. He uses them as steps of ascent into the presence of God; he enables us to see the crass history of the world as the rough rounds of the ladder on which angels are ascending and descending between us and God. When Christ came, it was inevitable, in the great effort of making the transition from ritualistic to spiritualistic worship, from our gifts to God to God's gifts to us, that the very most should be made of the religious ideas that had been gained in connection with sacrifices, and that sacrificial forms should be stretched to their utmost significance. All the light that was in the relation must be diligently used to open the way into perfect light, and to help the mind to discern the real dependence of the two systems that sought to compass the one essential thing, reconciliation. It would also as inevitably happen that the old bottles would not contain the new wine, and that in their unwise use they would be burst and the wine spilt. The injunction of Christ was very much in point, and very earnest, Put new wine in new bottles. When Christ is made a sacrifice to conciliate God, we have poured the new vintage into the old vessels. When Christ is a sacrifice, a sacrifice on the divine side to conciliate and guide men, and draw them within the bonds of his love and wisdom, we have our new wine in fresh receptacles, and are rich with the gifts of Heaven. It is a matter largely of the historic sense how we understand the divine Revelation. Our narrow way of studying the divine record hides half its light and impedes the growing power which it is waiting to spread over the whole world. We should better understand the command to preach the Gospel to every creature, if we better understood the fact that the whole creation groaneth and travaileth together in pain until now, *waiting* for the adoption. The same inadequate ideas, the same obscure ways, the same hesitancy, uncertainty, and doubt in the presence of truth, have been and are everywhere among men. Yet along this line of revelation, of prophetic labor and constant transition, has the good seed, in the fulness of growth, broken forth with new flowers and new fruitage, and filled the earth with its fragrance. We are the heralds of a spiritual creation, the heralds of Christ. The dogmatic tendency must find correction in the historic spirit, or it becomes a laborious raking together of cast-off husks and empty stubble, as if these still held the living germs.

There is one more consideration closely associated with the inductive and historic temper which remains to be enforced on those who construct systematic theology, and that is the extent to which figurative language necessarily enters religious truth. There is no end to the confusion which has been occasioned in philosophy by the fact that language, first shaped in sensuous uses, has been transferred to intellectual relations only partly analogous to them. Thus the activities and laws of mind have been likened in inadmissible ways to those of matter. It has been found a most difficult thing—much of sound philosophy lies in it—to make a clean transition from matter to mind, from mind to matter, without losing the distinctive qualities of either, or breaking the union of the two. Men experience a similar difficulty in grasping the spiritual truth which lies enclosed in a concrete fact without carrying with it more of the limitations of the fact than belong to it. If they believe in spirits, they believe also in ghosts, and shortly huddle together with starting eyes while some horror of spiritualism passes before them. As the devils of old are represented as especially reluctant to leave the bodies of their victims, and, when driven out, as taking refuge in a herd of swine that ran down a steep place and perished in the sea, so men in their spiritual blindness cling closely to the familiar forms of things, and when forced loose from them, accept some still more inadequate image till they are swallowed up in a sea of sensuous relations. One may say of this sort of offence, that it must needs come, but woe unto the man by whom it cometh. We must approach spiritual things through physical things, but in the very instant of attaining them we must leave behind us the parted simile, as the growing plant the integument it has just broken.

The first example we adduce for enforcement is the doctrine of covenants. The discipline of the world is continuous. It cannot be otherwise. A higher stage of training, unsupported by a lower one, would fail at once. Transitions of any considerable importance in the moral world are very difficult of accomplishment. When the Jewish system and the Christian system are spoken of as distinct covenants, the one of works and the other of grace, we are not to understand the words in any exact way. They only express a new emphasis, a change of dominant idea, under which one and the same process goes forward. If we dwell upon this word covenant, transfer it from a broad to a narrow meaning, and assume that the gifts of God turn upon a distinct contract, we shall shortly find ourselves groping about among very limited and very arbitrary relations in a disappointing search for the divine mind. The figure is to be dealt with lightly, with delicate touch, and transcended at once. Nothing can be safely drawn from it as premises. We must hit away from it, as the bird strikes air with his wing as he rises.

In the Scriptural presentations of our relations to Christ we have a great variety of figurative expressions, all yielding some light, none yielding complete light. In order to receive what each has to impart, we must understand that all are inexact and inadequate. Christ is our ransom. He purchased us with his blood. We are redeemed, not by silver and gold, but with his precious blood. He was made a curse for us. He bore our sins on the tree. He is our passover; a sacrifice to God as a sweet-smelling savor. He is the lamb of God that taketh away the sins of the world. He was lifted up, as the serpent in the wilderness, that we might look unto him. He purges our consciences from dead works. We enter by him into the holiest. He is the end of the law for righteousness. To these relations are to be added those in which he is wont to speak of himself. He is the vine, the door, the shepherd, the light, the way, the truth, and the life. These images are to be all harmonized in the doctrine of Christ, and this harmony can only be secured when we make the ultimate truth, the relation of each mind to God, fundamental. This is the substance of that most compact and comprehensive assertion: "I am the way and the truth and the life."

Men have been very slow to see and accept the fact that the form of the punishment in the divine government is expressed under various figures, and declares nothing beyond the simple relation of sin and suffering. The tares are gathered and burned. The fishes are gathered, the good into vessels, and the bad are cast away. The rejected guests are cast into outer darkness, with wailing and gnashing of teeth. The wicked husbandmen are miserably destroyed.

The words of our Lord are especially figurative. Spiritual ideas are boldly rendered by all the familiar images of life, and the fortunes of the Kingdom of Heaven advance under the form of a wavering conflict between the forces of good and evil—good angels and evil angels working their will in the world. When the seventy return with joy, saying, "Lord, even the devils are subject unto us through thy name," he makes answer, "I beheld Satan as lightning fall from Heaven." When the Pharisees found fault with him for healing on the Sabbath day the woman who had a spirit of infirmity, he indignantly asks: "Ought not this woman, being a daughter of Abraham, whom Satan hath bound, lo, these eighteen years, be loosed from this bond on the Sabbath day?"[1] When Peter undertook to rebuke Christ, as he announced his coming crucifixion, he turned sharply upon his overbold disciple with the words: "Get thee behind me, Satan. Thou art an offence unto me."[2] Again, in anticipation of his unstable temper, he says to him: "Simon, Simon,

---

[1] Luke xiii., 16. [2] Matt. xviii., 23.

behold Satan hath desired to have you, that he may sift you as wheat."[1] The close interlock of all physical and spiritual relations in the mind of Christ is seen in his inquiry: "Whether is it easier to say to the sick of the palsy, Thy sins be forgiven thee, or to say, Arise, take up thy bed, and walk."[2]

The vivid and figurative character of the Scriptures, springing from the double necessity of imparting clearly obscure ideas, and of enforcing them, compels the wise student to use the utmost caution in subjecting these words of insight to verbal deductions. When Christ says that he speaks to the Jews in parables, because they seeing see not, and hearing hear not, neither do understand, he is emphasizing this very fact that religious ideas become verbal and wholly obscure when they sink into a fixed terminology, and that they gain color again only by bringing them back to the events of life. Divine principles play, like lights and shadows, among things, and must be there caught in their true significance before we can safely systematize them.

Is it not, for example, more rational to suppose that the doctrine of evil spirits is a figurative rendering of the conflicts of sin, rather than a literal statement of facts? That man is in any way subject to agents of evil, hidden from him, waylaying him, and far superior to him in craftiness, is a supposition wholly incongruous with a sound interpretation of daily life. The possession by evil spirits was a belief figuratively true and literally untrue. A profitable discussion of the real nature of these manifestations was not yet prepared for in the experience of the Jew, or in his methods of thought. The moral force of the events was more deeply felt

---

[1] Luke xxii., 31.   [2] Mark ii., 9.

under the popular notion than it would have been under a new idea inadequately imparted. Christ submitted his methods to the circumstances under which the truth was to be urged. A confining of attention to primary principle was essential for their immediate apprehension, and for the apprehension of all secondary facts in due order.

We are now prepared to see both the dangers of dogma and its office in Christian experience. Dogmatism claims a certainty of results and an absoluteness of authority quite foreign to the circumstances of the case. In doing this it embarrasses the religious life, places the emphasis at the wrong point, and fortifies it with a perverse temper. Truth is to minister to emotion, emotion is to inform conduct, and conduct is to reinterpret truth. Life thus becomes a circuit of living experiences. The arrest of this movement in its first step checks all growth. It is flexible truth which subserves the purposes of progress. Inflexible truth begins at once to lose power. The human mind is exceedingly limited in its attainments. This weakness is to be corrected by growth; but growth involves the freedom of change. This principle prevails everywhere in the world of living things. Dogmatism contravenes this law, and contravenes it precisely where it should have its fullest authority. The spirit of dogmatism, by anticipating growth, comes to stand directly in the way of it, and that in a region in which all things remain to be won.

Doctrines, as the product of the reflective process, are especially unfit to be made the primary centres of union among men. Division, discrimination, careful emphasis, belong pre-eminently to the analytic and synthetic movement of mind. The very purpose of this systematizing process is to give particulars their due weight; and it often results in assigning them excessive weight. Not till we return to conduct and the sympathetic feelings that it calls out do we find the currents of human life running together again and overcoming all erratic tendencies. It is the union of action which corrects the division of thought. If men are discriminating they cannot rally to a creed as they can to an undertaking.

The creed also, as a fixed term in the life of a church, has helped to deaden its activity. A decay of piety disproportioned to the decay of doctrine is, in any long series of years, so universal a fact in every religious organization as to have the force of a law. This result is in part due to the separation occasioned between belief and conduct by a closed creed; the failure of the former to control the latter, and the failure of the latter to correct the former. The living movement is arrested by dividing its terms. A reform in action always means one in belief also. It thus happens that, in periods of dormant faith, piety passes into pietism, an artificial quickening of feeling aside from the discipline of duties. The entire life thus becomes artificial because of the remote and visionary nature of its first terms in systematic faith. From this feverish activity there is a slow decline under the gravitation of sin.

Sharp theological discussion not only begets hopeless division along slight lines of cleavage; it occasions much bitterness of feeling, and springs up in the practical world as thorns and thistles. There is scarcely a sadder chapter in human history—one of mingled regret, disgust, and despair—than that of theological discussion. The light that is in these heavens serves only to make them the more lurid and portentous. We restore our faith by remembering how tentative, obscure, and partial are all the stages of growth.

Yet religious doctrine expresses an inevitable tendency of thought and subserves a most important and undeniable purpose. A current so strong and deep and constant as this implies a large territory back of it, which is its occasion. The object subserved by dogma is a complex one of life and of philosophy. All sound philosophy is a philosophy of life, and all large life issues in philosophy. A philosophy of some sort must be, as a conscious or a latent term, back of all rational action. Our only protection against that which is weaker is that which is stronger; against superstition is faith, against negation is affirmation, against sinking into ignorance is rising into knowledge. We must do the best we can, as our only safety against doing worse than we might.

The human mind, by its upward bent, pushes into the light, and the highest light into which it can grow is this very light of a philosophy of life, a theory of the Divine Presence, a programme of the eternal procedure in the moral world. To underrate the value of this work is insensate, so insensate that no matter how wise those may be who fall into this error, how great the scorn they bestow on this inquiry, men are sure to return to it, and the chances are that these agnostics themselves will, in one way or another, at one time or another, occupy themselves with it. They do not escape the fascination of these profound questions by denying their fitness. If metaphysics is a wallow in the spiritual world, it is one to which men, no matter how often washed by science, are ever returning.

We have no patience with the spurious knowledge—spurious in this one particular—which decries the highest, most ultimate, most inevitable form of inquiry. Systematic theology, while it has no premises which entitle it to final conclusions, has abundantly the material of search, and deepens thought and enriches feelings beyond other forms of investigation. It has an irresistible fascination for the vigorous intellect, and draws men into its vortex in the very act of turning from it. When men fully apprehend that life involves a philosophy of life, and that the largest, most self-conscious life involves the presence of this philosophy in the mind as a distinct term of thought, they will understand the office of systematic theology—a careful inquiry into the ultimate relations of conduct.

No investigation is more important, because none covers more comprehensively all the terms of experience, none is more practical, because, while modified by all the conditions of life, it brings, in turn, constant modification to them.

This, indeed, is what we have been urging, that induction should unite itself to deduction in theology, that principles should interpret themselves by the facts that come under them, that the events of life should contain and confirm our revelation of God, and that we should see that from the beginning his method of instruction has been empirical and historical. We are quite right in deducing great truths from that exceptionally clear and significant record of facts—the Bible; we mistake only when we suppose it to be different in its truths from other sources of truth, and diverse in its record from the record we ourselves are making under the same overshadowing providence. The second coming of Christ, his daily access to us, is not less significant than his first coming.

Natural theology underlies revealed theology. However numerous and explicit the principles we trace to the Scriptures, they all rest back on, and help to bring to light, the truths incorporated in the constitution of things. Whatever may be the source of light, that which it illuminates and enlivens is the universe about us. Light and the things revealed lie in the closest interaction— neither is intelligible without the other.

CHAPTER IV.

PIETISM.

THE religious life, as a higher life, a life under a wider range of motives, and motives less immediate and tangible than those of the appetites and passions, seems vague and remote to most men. They find difficulty in laying hold of it, and turning it into palpable convictions and suitable actions. There has been, in consequence of this uncertain touch in spiritual things, a constant effort to give outline and definition to religious life by prescribed duties, explicit professions, and strong conventional feelings. This tendency to narrow, and at the same time to intensify, religious experience, is what we understand by pietism. It is piety expressed vigorously, but in a circumscribed form, that is deemed distinctively religious. The pietist is a man of ardent devotion to distinctively religious duties, with an intense form of character colored by supersensuous convictions, and with a burning desire to inspire his own sentiments in others. In pietism the religious life is gathered, like sunlight passing through a lens, into a heated centre, rather than diffused, like sunlight in the atmosphere, over the entire field of action. Pietism is a familiar fact in all forms of faith. It arises inevitably from the narrowness of human thought in connection with a desire more completely to express one's obedience to truth. It has belonged, in a great variety of forms, to the Christian Church almost from the beginning.

The first extended and striking manifestation of it was asceticism. The ascetic gave shape to his Christian experience in arbitrary self-denial, and with sufferings which were not associated with the performance of any duty. No specific good came either to himself or to others by his self-imposed inflictions; except as they were regarded as the expression of religious feeling. Religious devotion, turning aside from simple and direct labor in doing good, devised for itself a severe method of discipline, with no basis in nature and no merit of service to mankind. Asceticism was an irrational and melancholy perversion of Christian self-denial, and yet was not wholly without value, simply because it sprang from the higher incentives and reacted on them. It was life, though a deformed and diseased one. Asceticism, in its squalor, solitude, and self-devised sufferings, was not merely a failure to apprehend and perform social duties, a substitution of meaningless inflictions for the labors of a divine beneficence, it was a trespass, and often a grievous trespass, on the physical, the intellectual, and the spiritual powers. The mind was filled with visions, neither pure nor peaceful, neither wholesome nor corrective. The religious life suffered profound misapprehension and profound perversion. This distortion belonged to asceticism not merely in its extreme forms, but in its entire spirit; to all self-denial accepted for any other object than real service. It misconceived the will of God and our duty to him, and put in place of actions spiritually beautiful, deformed and frightful ones. It is a diabolical spectacle to see men inflict pain on each other as a religious duty; it is a spectacle of infatuation and folly hardly less depressing to see them inflict sufferings on themselves as a divine discipline.

Yet so strongly is this tendency associated with devotion, that it is constantly reappearing, and assuming some new phase. Many, especially in the Catholic Church, express a temper of self-denial in needless sufferings; as if the thing called for were not a rational surrender of immediate pleasure in behalf of an adequate end, but simply the surrender itself. The sin against reason in asceticism is complete. Wise suffering is endured for the sake of limiting evil and removing pain; ascetic inflictions are undergone as a voluntary enlargement of pain. Not only does evil carry with it pain, pain carries with it evil, in wasting productive power and impoverishing the spiritual affections. Although the contention against pain in the world is subordinate to that against evil, the two forms of strife must go on together, and share the same fortunes. To introduce needless pain is to give sin needless provocation.

The hold which this form of pietism retains on the ardent, spiritual mind was recently illustrated in the narrative of Clare Vaughan. Her devotion is spoken of as one which gives us "a standard by which to measure the Christian life and the high aspiration of Catholic faith." "Even her childhood was marked by an enthusiastic love of Christ—such a love that her companions discovered with pain that it was really filling her mind, almost to the eclipse of her devotion to them,—and also by a passion for self-inflicted sufferings endured to prove this deep love which seems to those who are not Roman Catholics a strange form of devotion, and one that contrasts very remarkably with the brightness and sweetness of Clare Vaughan's disposition." "Her love of mortification was such that nothing she saw or came across failed to suggest some means of torturing or annoying her unfortunate body. How well I remember one day when we were returning from a village in the neighborhood. We happened to be passing through a stubble-field, and breaking off suddenly from what she had been talking about, she cried, ' I have a splendid idea! Suppose we take off our shoes and stockings and walk barefoot through the stubble-field!' It was no sooner said than done, and I can see now the calm enjoyment with which Clare walked up and down those cruel many-bristling thorns, followed by the sympathetic shrieks of her cowardly companion, who very soon resumed shoes and stockings." [1]

How came asceticism to arise as a pietistic tendency in the Christian Church? and what has been its effects, good and evil, on our apprehension of the spirit of Christ? Asceticism gave at once that definite, tangible expression to the religious life which men desired. It satisfied the wish of the devout to do something as an instant and adequate outcome of feeling, and to separate themselves by bold lines of division from the irreligious. The notoriety which attended on extreme asceticism carried with it a mingled flavor of good and evil. The devotee, by extravagant self-denial, might gratify the very pervasive and subtle feeling of vanity, and might also, to his own apprehension, extend religious truth.

The conditions under which Christian life was developed in earlier centuries were such as to favor asceticism. It was not easy to impose religious truth in wholesome forms on the minds of men. The obstructions to conceiving and expressing the right temper were very great. It was natural, therefore, to feel, that as one could not save the world, he must save himself by a sepa-

[1] *The Spectator*, October 29, 1887.

ration from it. In this isolation, the discipline of useful labors being lost, its place was supplied by artificial exactions, and these were increased with the increase of the spirit of self-denial. The movement, having missed the guidance of facts, found no limits within itself. The desire of redeeming one's soul took the place of the desire of redeeming the world. Thus the relation of these two ideas, the salvation and the renovation of the spirit, was hopelessly confused. The saving the soul came to mean the rescuing of the man from the future consequences of sin rather than immediate purification. The future was to be won more or less at the cost of the present, not by and with it. Asceticism favored this confusion of thought, and grew up with it. The maimed character of the life the devotee was at the time leading was not the point of attention, but the effects of his action on a future life. The moment we make this distinction, darkness and error enter rapidly. The continuity of life is lost. Our exertions are turned into a kind of spiritual gymnastics of whose value we have no immediate test. They are undertaken for obscure, remote objects, and must find their justification in them. Everything hinges upon our theory of salvation, and as long as this holds good in the mind, we may wisely increase our spurious acts of self-sacrifice. The man who is striving to help men in the world, who is trying to improve the world as the abode of men, has the present fruits of his efforts to enlarge and correct his judgments; but he who is struggling to save souls, in this narrow sense, decides on the success of his measures under the same artificial ideas that have led him to enter on them. He meets, therefore, with nothing to expose his failures, for his thought and method are fanciful throughout.

A very intelligent workman, whose proclivities were

skeptical, once said to me, that if Christians would cease their efforts to save the souls of men and try to save their bodies, they would do much better. In this assertion we have the complimentary error of the mistake of asceticism, the expectation of securing physical progress in separation from spiritual improvement. The two are so interwoven in the divine method, that neither can be pursued successfully, for any length of time, aside from the other. Stalwart righteousness means stalwart strength, and demands, in its proper expression, large physical and intellectual appliances. The beauty of the world loses its most fitting ministrations without righteousness, and righteousness misses its ineffable perfection, if it has no mastery of the means by which it is to declare itself. The Kingdom of Heaven is embodied righteousness, righteousness that builds up society, enriches and beautifies it. The ascetic, aiming to save his own soul by self-imposed discipline, in separation from the world about him, fails to understand rightly in what salvation consists. The soul can only be saved in connection with men, as its salvation lies in deepened, widened, quickened affections. Love must have before it the field of love, or it can gain no new power. We might as well expect bodily strength without bodily action, as spiritual strength without contact with spiritual interests. A man saves himself in saving others. Inflictions that subserve no purposes of reconstruction among men arise from a perversion of thought and still further extend it. Paul says: "I rejoice in my sufferings for you, and fill up that which was wanting in the sufferings of Christ." But these were sufferings in behalf of others, and made necessary by the exigencies of the case. God's school is one of suffering, but not one of wasted suffering. Its aim is to overcome suffering in behalf of ourselves and others.

The discipline of suffering lies chiefly in the earnestness and wisdom of the effort to eliminate it. Love animates this effort, and all the affections gather in its path. What more manifest spiritual sophism than a gratuitous infliction of suffering on ourselves, when it is, with us, a constant duty to relieve the sufferings of others? While it is not the very substance of righteousness to escape pain, it is its manifest glory that it does escape it. We should have hardly fallen so readily into this error of self-mortification, if we had not become accustomed to look on the sufferings of Christ as arbitrary.

Yet asceticism has played an important part in the spiritual improvement of the world. It offers another illustration of the familiar fact, that the road to truth is always one of error. A temper of abnegation may be present in pietism, and help to give the spirit that mastery over itself which is an essential in righteousness. Asceticism, when it is associated with beneficence, makes a very strong appeal to the imagination of men. Even that which is preposterous in it adds to the impression. The purely voluntary character of the suffering becomes its merit, and enhances its force as a mastery of spiritual ideas. The simplicity of truth is often less efficacious with men than some striking exhibit made under an error allied to the truth.

In asceticism, the spirit does itself a violence in breaking away from dominant, sensuous ideas. It treats its own most needful members as if they were enemies, and maims itself in seeking liberty, as the wild animal may pluck itself from the trap with the loss of a limb. Nobility of purpose is here united with folly of method, and often, in the balance of effects, carries the day. The living plant triumphs over a bleak climate.

Yet the error of method is here to bear with it its disastrous entail. The thoughts are narrowed, the affections impoverished, and labor made unfruitful by a procedure transverse to the grace of God, not parallel with it. If one does not rise above asceticism, by asceticism religion is slowly converted into fanaticism, ever more barren, deformed, and hateful. We must expect error, but we must also look for the power to shake it off. The prayer and fasting of the New Testament may easily be made to grow into asceticism. They need, in use, the interpretation of reason under adequate ends. They are good so far as they purify and strengthen the mind without diverting it from its true labors or weakening it in them. The simple fact which remains at the centre of the divine method, that body and mind can only work successfully in the closest union, is a law to grace as much as it is to labor.

Pietism arises very frequently in reaction against a self-indulgent phase of religious life. The asceticism of St. Francis and the poverty which he enjoined on his followers were distinguishing traits in a corrupt period. The Franciscans thus drew attention and addressed the popular conscience in a new and direct way. The spirit of their work was expressed and aided by this voluntary self-denial. It is often easier, and for the moment more effective, to transcend the line of wise and proportionate action than it is to reach and maintain it.

But the Franciscans did not escape the taint of thought and feeling attendant on this enforced poverty. The bitter hostility between the spirituals, who adhered to the doctrine in its extreme form, and the conventuals, who softened it to suit changing conditions, and the cruel persecution of the former, were some of the fruits of this early excess in the life and spirit of St. Francis. The acts and garments which marked the ascetic temper became with many of his disciples things of fundamental importance. Every irrational action helps to destroy the balance of thought, and to turn the indomitable energy of a devout mind into self-assertion. The stronger the impulse with which we are dealing, the greater our need of sober judgment.

A second form of pietism is ritualism, when pushed beyond its simple disciplinary service. The need of a rite arises from ignorance and weakness. It puts upon the mind a method of worship, because the mind cannot advantageously supply its own method. Or a system of rites unites men in worship, and prevents a wasteful collision of forms. Where the spirit of God is, there is liberty, because there is the capacity to use liberty. Rites will be gross and cumbersome in the degree in which those who employ them are barren in spiritual life. The complicated temple worship, the innumerable bloody sacrifices of the Jewish service, were very coarse expressions of our relations to God. The sensuous element in them was large, and easily overpowered their spiritual import. They were adapted to a people gross of heart and stiff of neck. The first terms in the spiritual training of an unspiritual people must necessarily be remote from the inner life of faith. Ritualism arises in accommodation to a sensuous temper. It gives an artificial approach to God, when the soul is failing of ready access to him. This relation of rites to religion implies a disparagement of them, and yet it involves their immense value in the history of the world. One can hardly use a liturgy, permeated with spiritual insight, without becoming enamored of it. It so touches in purity the best thoughts of men, so enriches itself by association, so gathers into a swift, songful stream of utterance the feelings of all who unite in it, that one seems to have found, having wandered in paths remote, the highway to Heaven.

But the pietistic spirit, the spirit of concentration and excess, easily lays hold of ritualism, as especially suited to its purposes. The ritual is made minute and vigorous. The religious life is sharply distinguished by means of it, and duty rapidly becomes the faithful use of means, not the wise winning of ends. A ritual is a ready way of giving outward form to religious action, and consoling the mind with results that are immediate and visible. For the ultimate up-shot of the method, it can fall back on the spirit of mysticism, on the inscrutable and the divine. If we are to judge the world by God's declaration of it in science, it is, in construction, profoundly opposed to mysticism; if we are to judge of it by man's exposition of it in religion, it lapses readily, in many ways and places, into obscure and fanciful connections. Man is always practically struggling with the question, how to satisfy the sensuous tendencies and the spiritual tendencies of the mind without a decisive victory of either, without the incorporation of both in a higher life. A ritual is a short answer to this inquiry. When this answer has been made, any extra pressure of the higher sentiments shows itself in pietism, in restored, enlarged, and enforced rites that will retain more or less of their disciplinary character, according to the disposition of the person who makes use of them. If the rite does not steadily raise us above the rite, our observance of it will become an increasing obstruction to vision, casting a deeper and deeper shadow on the real duties of life.

The form of pietism most immediately interesting to us is that which is more frequently associated with Protestant forms of faith—the pietism of intensified, religious sentiment. We need say nothing of the pietism of rigorous doctrine, for that has been sufficiently considered as dogmatism. Religious feeling often leads the mind to enforce a creed, aside from any intellectual apprehension of it. The movement of the mind is not pure and colorless, but turbid with mistaken feeling. The sentiments add themselves as so much weight to the thoughts, and thus enhance their momentum in a disastrous way. It is this emotional element, uncontrolled of reason, that converts belief into dogmatism, and disturbs the composure of the spirit.

But there is a pietism of intensified feeling disconnected from the creed. The emotions are laboriously called out and carefully cherished as containing the distinguishing terms of a religious experience without relation to their immediate connection with well-directed effort. The feelings are thus sought after and fed out of connection with their vital dependencies and purposes. Our convictions of sin, our sense of the nearness of God, or of the duty of prayer, or of the value of a religious experience, are kept alive by constantly returning to them, and by an assiduous effort to make them, in an intense form, habitual. They thus become direct products of will, instead of the indirect fruits of conduct. The religious life is identified with these feelings, and their maintenance is made a leading purpose. The saints of Protestant churches are quite likely to have a decisive tinge of this form of pietism. Saintship is associated with the religious sentiments. Devotion, consecration, separation from the world, are its designations, and may cover an exalted yet an artificial state of mind. These experiences miss the true breadth of life, the real power of the spirit. They bear a narrow remedial character, rather than one of wide renovation and growth. If our bodily members are sinking into torpor, if the circulation is partially checked, we may restore this, certainly, by friction. But the results so secured are quite distinct from the vigor of the entire body, and are by no means to be substituted for it. Religious feelings that are not the spontaneous out-flow of a noble and useful life, feelings that are cherished as in themselves an experience, that special experience we term spiritual, may also be the products of an intellectual friction, and lead us to carry this movement cure into all departments of faith. Our Christian churches are very much influenced in their efforts by pietism, and religion is not so much a large and wise government of life as certain obscure experiences superinduced upon it.

A rare form of pietism, which one is least disposed to criticise, but does well to understand, is the entire and direct devotion of one's property to religious work. It has offered itself in religious orders as the vow of poverty. This form of pietism, while lacking that completeness and breadth of motives which belong to true spirituality, may very well show great moral power. A manifest and absolute subordination of lower to higher motives gives to the latter a sense of reality which the popular mind is sure to appreciate. This consecration puts that in the foreground which is in the foreground, and errs only in not sufficiently supporting it with all the beauty and large invitation that lie in the rear of true holiness.

The motives of life are very various and very complex, and should render each other, in the development of virtue, constant and extended support. The best impulses take on harsh and barren phases unless they are finding their way among the manifold forms of a complete life. The social and the spiritual incentives which gather about the acquisition and expenditure of property bring very extended, forceful, and needful motives to action. They are wrought thoroughly into the constitution of the world, of man and of society. Progress certainly needs their aid, and will be found closely associated with them. While it is a noble thing to push right through minor interests and enter heartily into larger ones that lie beyond, it is a more proportionate method and, in the progress of years, effective one, to gather up in a purified form all accessory incentives, and to unite, on the broad basis of the actual world, those forces which must ultimately enter into society, support, and nourish it. That mastery of wealth which retains its varied uses, which enables its possessor, with no separation between himself and other men, no loss of sympathy with them, to work effectively on every plane of effort with every worthy impulse, higher and lower, to prosper the present labors as well as the future hopes of life, to gather to the spiritual front the pleasure and beauties of existence in their divine order, to reflect with happy forecast the multiplied enjoyments we bestow so lavishly on our conception of Heaven—that mastery is certainly far better than an abnegation which puts away effort and temptation because they are too hard for us.

In the long work of redemption and construction all the resources of the world must come into play, and we do well to learn how to hold them together in the very outset; how to build them together in a social structure well supported within and without by all modes of dependence and bonds of union. This extreme consecration, bearing the narrow cast of pietism, in its effort to win the higher in oversight of that which is lower, finds really no encouragement in the example of the Master.

The young man who came to our Lord with the inquiry, "What shall I do to be saved?" was met with the command, "Sell all that thou hast, and give to the poor"; because only thus could a thickly woven veil of spiritual sophistries be rent through, and the light be admitted to his bewildered mind. As an example, it stands quite by itself, and testifies to its exceptional character. A giving that overlooks in the giver the appropriate conditions of economic and social progress, must always suffer abatement in its force of example. Men instantly feel that the method is not a universal one. They, therefore, are content to regard it as more exceptional than it really is. An attitude toward the use of property, which appreciates all its ministrations,—outward, inward, and upward—is that more rare and noble thing—the divine mind, in its plentitude of methods and breadth of motives. To know how to possess the world is to know how to possess Heaven,—is to convert it into Heaven.

Pietism is closely associated with two points of belief that narrow our relations to the world. The first of these is that conversion involves a sudden, decisive change of character, and may be present more or less aside from the slow gains of obedience. Daily experience is misinterpreted in the establishment of this theory of an immediate transformation, and sentiments—the conventional sentiments of pietism—are accepted as the sound and sufficient currency of a new life. In the degree in which the changes of character are taken out from under the ordinary laws of mind, and consequences are looked for which have no sufficient antecedents in conduct, shall we find ourselves afloat in thought, and ready to receive mystic expressions of feeling as signs of the divine favor. The seed sown on light soil, and sown among thorns, perishing by the heat or choked by the weeds, becomes a type of that pietism which arises from the ready admission of supernaturalism into the sources of conduct. If the elements of character may enter suddenly, and out of relation to the bulk of action, then may we possibly be able to induce fortunate sentiments by some special point of view painfully maintained. If, however, we are put in connection with the entire world, with its innumerable wants, for the very end of giving us terms of discipline; if the breadth of sound conduct bears some proportion to the breadth of these its enclosing relations; if the solidity of character is incident to firm repose on these same supporting facts; if favorable changes of character must arise by temperate and wise action under them; and if the only sufficient proof of meeting the divine will is the enlargement of the divine love among men, then this pietism which gives an in-door culture to a few selected and artificial sentiments is a mistake, and stands in very partial harmony with the broad and patient thought of God. We must understand by conversion, before we can pursue it aright, a steady turning toward a larger and more gracious life, a slow putting forth, under more comprehensive feelings, of bud, leaf, flower, and fruit in a Kingdom of Heaven, beautiful with an amplitude all its own.

The second impression which leads to pietism is one entertained much in the face of the words of Christ, the feeling that salvation has chief reference to another life. We allow the larger interests of that life to stand over against the immediate interests of this life, and so put the two in conflict in their action on us. These interests, on either hand, are part and parcel of the same thing. The salvation of another life is in continuation of the salvation of this life, and is reached through it. It is not sufficient to look upon conduct and character as means to an end, salvation; they are the very substance of salvation. The Kingdom of Heaven is within us. We are in the midst of God's redemptive grace, and have no occasion to forecast a future in which that grace shall declare itself. The Kingdom we labor for, and of which by our labors we are made partakers, is a Kingdom that overlaps the world. Thy will be done in earth as it is in Heaven. When we strengthen ourselves against the failures of well-doing by the assurance of ultimate success, we do wisely; but when we console ourselves with feeble things, flattered by a promise of better ones beyond the limits of our own action, we are simply nursing our indolence. Spiritual life comes under the conditions of all life, and we maintain our hold on the future by our hold on the present.

Pietism overlooks, or underestimates, this living continuity, this organic character of truth, and nourishes expectations in contradiction of the terms of their fulfilment. It is thus negligent in securing these terms. Our belief in the blessings of the future is superinduced on the ills of the present, not to make us diligent in correcting them, but to render us patient in tolerating them—a patience that approaches contentment, when these ills are spiritual, not physical, ones. Pietism often intensifies feelings which divert us from the very process of their realization. We misconceive the evils under which we are laboring, and misconceive their remedy. We fall into the very pervasive fallacy that the modification of things is more significant than that of persons; that the patient, spiritualizing discipline to which we are subjected is in a measure superfluous. Life is present in the degree in which love is present, and in that degree only. The world is the school of love. Miss the lesson, and we miss the Heaven which lies in learning it.

We propose, as a theme of social worship, " God's unspeakable gift, do we possess it ? " In considering it, the mind is confused between the winnings of the present life and the rewards of a future life, between naturalism and supernaturalism. With a pietistic temper we throw the balance of hope on the least tangible term. We are to have what we now have not. It is as if we should strive to rest, not on the foot already planted, but on that which is raised for forward movement. Our poise in the spiritual world is in the present ; from this support we must make our cast into the future. God's unspeakable gift is the power and opportunity of immediate growth.

Pietism is sure to accompany a supernaturalism in any way separated from naturalism. It is a belief, in one or more particulars, in such a separation ; a waiting to realize results that transcend the connections of experience. It is a kind of ecstasy made to take the place of sober thought, and though it may not be altogether ill-placed or ineffectual, it cannot, with strength and safety, attain to the sufficient and peaceful fruits of righteousness. Pietism contains the fallacy of a search after effects without sufficient causes—after sentiments not fully sustained by the circumstances which give occasion to them. It is not in harmony with those many stages of growth, those untiring processes of consolidation, those innumerable steps of diffusion, under labor, by which God leads us into a kingdom, comprehensive of all, and of all the interests of each. Pietism, the feverish activity of spiritual life at a few points, and its strange torpor at many points, is the outcome of a mode of thought that overlooks, somewhat, the fixed dependence of events on each other, and expects, at some stage of progress, to rise suddenly, like a bird in the air, and leave great spaces behind it. Pietism is the intoxication of piety, and, like intoxication, sobers down into weakness and fear.

This temper exists in every measure, from the slight extravagance of healthy activity to the abnormal conceptions of extreme asceticism. While pietism finds its occasion in our misapprehension of the processes of grace, in our unwise understanding of the relations of the present to the future and of God's gifts to our own activity, it finds its incentives in desires which belong to us as mere children, wayward and ignorant in spiritual things. A disposition to compromise is the inevitable outcome of strong, conflicting feelings. What takes place in a body of men with divided interests takes place in each man with divided sentiments. No far-reaching reform has come to any people without passing through many phases of pitiful compromise, and being pushed by means of them to a final issue. Such an evil as intemperance is plucked up, like a noxious, spreading plant, root by root, patch by patch. Religion demands that a new centre should be taken, and all thought and action be rearranged from it. Man neither fully sees this demand, nor readily assents to it. The alterations of character are slow and partial. Attention is concentrated on single forms of experience, and so we have pietism. Pietism is a compromise between sin and holiness by which something is conceded and something saved, by which the religious life is held back from the entire field of conduct, but, in compensation, is allowed to rule here and there with peculiar rigor. Men, in dealing with spiritual motives, are encountering ideas more or less alien to their experience, and so they give them partial, distorted, and extreme expression. The spiritual life is a struggle, and thus for a long time a compromise, between conflictiong tendencies.

A second occasion of pietism is the desire of men to reach quickly tangible results. Pure spiritualism is too remote, too broad, too supersensible for their successful pursuit. A narrower difference, a more immediate distinction, even if it be a superficial one, pleases them better. Pietism meets this feeling. The ascetic, whatever else he is or is not, is separate from the world. The ritualist is at once distinguishable in his ways and his worship. The pietist of sentiment is divisible immediately from his fellows by his strong and pungent phraseology. These distinctions enhance the impression that the children of God are, as indeed they ought to be, a peculiar people. The delight, on the one side, in a visible result, and the blindness, on the other, which obscures the real qualities of the Kingdom of Heaven, give occasion to pietism, as a short-hand method of recording tendencies that men have not yet the grace to write at large. We discern superficial differences far more quickly than profound ones, and stumble on for a long time among the lengthened shadow of things still remote from us. We have not reached the foot of the mount of vision, much less climbed its slope.

The evils of pietism are partial, open to correction, and inseparably associated with many gains. Pietism is an inadequate, transitional form of life, and may give way to one more pervasive. It delays us in understanding the religious spirit. A growing comprehension of that spirit, not as one which seeks peculiar terms in experience, but as one which handles familiar terms with more insight, will drive back pietism, point by point, and will substitute for the feverish action of one set of faculties the measured action of all the faculties. It is for the sake of the religious life, its right apprehension, its true extension, that we censure pietism as an insufficient expression of the divine mind.

Pietism is almost inevitable among the ignorant, and yet they especially suffer from it. One approaches an average man in whom the upward tendency of thought has been repressed by the urgent wants, coarse desires, and superficial conventionalisms of a narrow experience. He is of the earth earthy. His affections are of the natural, and not of the spiritual, order. The forces which construct society are not thought of; no personal or social ideal is present to the imagination. He walks by the sight of the eyes, almost as much so as an animal, only with a wider range of objects. One wishes to awaken religious ideas in such a person, or impart to him a decisive religious impulse. He finds himself at great disadvantage in attempting it. No common ground, common vocabulary, common experience, lie between them. His words sink into weak moral truisms, and carry no weight. It is hardly possible to reach such a man without some degree or form of pietism. Some impressions must be thrown out of proportion in order that they may gain the appearance of strength. Emphasis must be excessive, that the truth may offer itself as at all emphatic. Such a man identifies religion with religious professions, religious actions, religious distinctions; marks with which he is familiar, and without which he misses the lessons they contain.

Yet such a person suffers very much from pietism. He does not comprehend the religious force of what you say till you use the right phrase, and when the conventional expression is employed, he readily lapses into a narrow, sanctimonious form of thought which has in it very little renovating power. He can recognize religion only in one way, and so when the recognition comes it is of very restricted value. If we believe that what God requires is the blood of bulls and goats, that the pietistic sentiment is the substance of piety, then the grace, naturalness, and largeness of salvation will remain hidden from us.

Religion needs to renew its speech constantly; it calls for more direct forms of thought, for less conventional and more spiritual modes of expression. A first office of the religious life is to give light, light to words, light to actions, light to all the straight and winding paths that lead upward, light that discloses the living gifts and manifold beauties of the ways of God. Pietism fails in its own revelation and fails as a revelation. It is a disguise and a restriction, in one degree or another, of the grace of God. Those who are spiritually minded are predestined of God to beget a pure, bracing spiritual atmosphere, which re-endows, with its vitalizing energies, all the higher powers of men. The close air and mal-odors of an unventilated room are not more hostile to robust health, than are the set phrases and meagre experiences of pietism to spiritual strength, and full fraternity in the Kingdom of Heaven. The deep evil of pietism is that it misapprehends the religious life which it seeks to propagate. The divine love struggles first with disobedience, and then with the narrow forms of obedience that replace it.

As itself a restriction of life, pietism modifies all our methods of presenting life in the household and the Church. It is hardly necessary to say, that an effort to correct a method does not necessarily involve an oversight of the gains that have accompanied it, or of its unavoidable character as a transitional phase in development. Life is always busy in taking down that which it itself has built up. Any particular form of pietism arises from the defective conceptions of truth on the part of those who teach and of those who are taught. It is an obscure, spiritual product which can only be changed slowly as the result of increasing insight. A sweeping condemnation of the modes of instruction, at any one time prevalent, arises from a superficial apprehension of the force of the facts with which they are associated, and a presumptuous hope of an easy correction of fact and theory together. Our choice, in the world's progress, lies more in the rapidity of changes, than it does in the steps of change. Wise criticism is chiefly interested in the immediate possibilities of improvement, and emphasizes the partial failures of the past simply as giving the occasion of growth.

The instruction of the pulpit, when we consider how extended, constant, and earnest it is, is less efficacious than we might hope it to be. It is narrowed in its influence by the dogmatic, and, still more, by the pietistic, spirit. The pulpit aims at results, and produces results, far more limited than the wants of men. It does not address itself directly and broadly to these wants. Pietism is accepted as the germ of piety, and is enforced unhesitatingly as the substance of a religious life. But pietism is not piety in its expansive corrective phase, but in its phase of contraction. It is not putting truth to new uses, but holding it fast under a form of expression which is ready to be superseded. It is not the life that is advancing, but the life that will not give way.

When the dogmatic mind is met with the failure of truth to reach the masses of men, with the defection of the popular mind from religious ideas, it falls back at once on pietism. The old truths must be preached with more boldness and more conviction. Cold limbs must be warmed, and stiff limbs made limber, by friction. It fails to understand that this weakening of conviction is the inevitable outcome of truths which are not allowed to grow into and with the social activity that encloses them; that this lack of force is the very evil complained of, and cannot be corrected by lung power.

Pietism asserts that simple piety is to be sought after, and that it will bring with it, in due order, all moral virtues. And this assertion it makes in face of the fact that this very piety is pursued in separation from social, reformatory effort. The dogmatic temper fails to interpret piety in terms of human well-being, and yet affirms that piety will be so rendered in due order by those who possess it. Pietism lays more stress on the propagation, from person to person, of a given sentiment, than on the purification of that sentiment, till it becomes a medium of the divine mind; on conversion, than on the larger, more transcendent life for which it stands. It lays utmost emphasis on the beginnings of things, but is much less anxious that these first things should ripen into the fulness of the divine thought.

Pietism can exist, and frequently does exist, side by side with heinous forms of sin, without coming into distinct conflict with them; simply because it is substituting a narrow and more or less artificial experience for one of divinely ordered growth. It arrests truth, and allows the transgressions of men to arrest it, in its corrective power. It has not a sufficiently instant and urgent conception of the fulness of the Kingdom of Heaven to see the obstacles that lie in its path. It cannot open the conflict with evil at all points, because it has not drawn out its line of battle, and is overlapped on either hand.

Hence some great pervasive and consolidated wrong may exist in the presence of the Church, with hardly a perceptible power of rebuke on the part of the pulpit. The pulpit is occupied with pietism and not with politics, and men are busy with politics and not with pietism. The current phases of devotion are the staple of the pulpit, while intemperance, impurity, luxury, war, are off themes. What, for example, can be more hostile to the entire Christian temper than war, yet war never cost the Christian world more than it costs it to-day. The Church is powerless in the presence of this evil. The passions of men sweep by it, and overflow it, and pass through it, and hardly honor it with a ripple. The Church has no purchase, no leverage, against it. It nourishes pietism, but loses humanity. It preaches a truth that is to overcome transgression, and opens no conflict with the transgressions nearest to it. The truth ceases to be a sword and becomes a wand of office.

It will be felt at once that incessant attack on specific sins is ineffectual and inadmissible. This is, in a degree, true. But the difficulty does not lie so much in the absence of a constant, harassing, hand-to-hand fight, as in the fact that the forces of truth are not made to face the right way and the right things. The secrets of life that are contained in them remain hidden, and men do not distrust the fact. The habitual vision of faith does not lie across the plains of the Kingdom of Heaven. Men's ideals are remote from the purposes of God.

Great weight is attached to revivals, but a revival may easily be an objectionable phase of pietism, a new contraction of things infinitely too narrow already. What we wish to lay down are the lines of work along which the love of God is constantly passing into the lives of men, and building a kingdom of grace on earth. We have lost confidence in the assertion that this transition is sure to be made under the old method, and that we have only to abide by it. Pietism must break camp, dismiss its camp followers, and carry the glad tidings of a salvation that waits to sweep through every kingdom, physical, economic, social, pressing up toward a spiritual life that embraces them all, and redeems them all. All things travail together.

Pietism is a more definite product than piety, than a life enlarged through all its area to the bounds of grace. The preacher loves distinct results—results that take on a numerical expression. Pietism meets this desire. It lays down lines of division and walks within them. It builds a fence, and cultivates the enclosed area as the vineyard of God. Visible landmarks are set up in all directions, but the fields, white for the harvest, which Christ saw from the well at Sychar, still remain ungathered. Pietism is forgetful of the largest love, and hence of the fullest message, of Christ. It is not a gospel for every creature in every relation of life. It may be thought that we are trying to replace a pietism of reflection by one of action, a fanaticism of belief by one of labor, and so, like many another, fall short of the reposeful strength of the Kingdom of Heaven. Whether this is the issue or not will turn on the largeness of our discourse on truth, the number of the fountains of life from which we feed our life. It is catholicity of life that we urge, and philanthropy is only one of its modes of expression.

Pietism, by narrowing down the life of faith and weakening its inner force, helps to justify agnosticism. The grace of God must chiefly express itself in the moral world. If the spiritual world does not disclose a truly divine presence, that presence is lost to us. Religious conventionalisms, the shallowness of faith, its manifold errors, the deceptive way in which it clothes human passion with religious expression, the inadequacy of the ends it proposes, the formality of the means it uses, all help to disguise religious truth and give color to the assertion that faith is a tangle of obscure thought and perverted instincts, which can be unravelled into nothing worth having except a growing temper of humanity. This feeling is concisely, and somewhat contemptuously, expressed in the memoirs of Mark Pattison. At one time he was strongly influenced by the movement toward Catholicism which occurred at Oxford under the lead of Mr. Newman. He failed to take the decisive step, and later his interest in this experience and kindred ones wholly died away. He explains the fact by the "innutrition of the religious brain and the development of the rational faculties."[1]

This sarcasm would be of no moment did it not pierce to the quick a very weak point in religious development, this of pietism. Pietism is the fruit of a religious brain, crowded in development by special processes. It is opposed to the wide unfolding of rational faculties. When, therefore, the prevailing type of a religious experience is deeply tinctured with pietism, the rational sense of more rational men takes offense. They turn from it; they weary of it; they grow away from it. The pietist is ready with the answer that Christ necessarily brings offense. Is it this offense that Christ brings? I think not. It is hardness of thought and arrogance of feeling

[1] Page 208.

that he offends, not our rational sympathies, our wide-ranging humanity, our inner coherence of life. The agnostic will feel that, in scope of purpose, in justness and philanthropy of sentiment, John Stuart Mill had nothing to learn from the average Christian. Hence the profoundly unfortunate conclusion that the root of spiritual life lies not in religious faith, is not in a world knit through and through by spiritual forecast and spiritual favor, but in a humanity that is just opening up in development. Positivism is ready to steal the very office of faith in society. Humanity is put with freshness of power for piety, simply because piety is offered as pietism. Let us profoundly regret any religious spirit that through its self-imposed limitations stands rebuked in the presence of a positivism that sees more and feels more of the restless tide of human want, ebbing and flowing through this one moment of time, than do the servants of Christ, taught by all the centuries that come and go under the eye of God.

The most radical evil in pietism—the isolation of religious sentiment—is that it checks the development of manhood. Manhood, rightly understood, is the divine ideal embraced in individual and social life. We arrive at it, in the imperfect forms in which it offers itself to us, by a study of the facts of conduct, character, and social life. It is God's revelation in society of the beauty of moral excellence. The notion we entertain of manhood expresses our penetration into the spiritual scheme of things. Pietism arises from a narrow estimate of our more immediately personal relations, particularly those to God. These two things, manhood and piety, should concur, and do concur, so far as both are rightly grasped. The fitting expression of piety is manhood, a fulness of response to the duties that lie upon us and the affections which surround us. The partial conceptions we are forming of manly character we often designate as honor; while the correspondingly defective notions which arise in connection with piety are the innumerable forms of pietism. These two partial presentations more or less supplement each other in their defects. Honor lacks the patience and devotion of piety, and pietism misses the immediate insight into secular relations which manhood enforces. While true character embraces both piety and manhood, they easily antagonize each other, first, by establishing different standards of excellence, and later, by scorning the virtues not contained in their own ideal. Hence the two tempers may settle down into mutual misapprehensions and repulsions. We suffer from cross-vision in the spiritual world, and have difficulty in bringing together our images of excellence in one clearly outlined object. We have been accustomed to separate between our earthward and heavenward seeking. It is the office of righteousness to unite the two in an ideal character, commanding the whole circle of virtues; those which adjust us to the immediate conditions of conduct, and those by which we understand its real trend.

The partial separation between the manly and the religious type of character—a separation that is increased by every phase of pietism—has brought with it conspicuous evils. The standard of honor is frequently more narrow than that of pietism, and is maintained with a like dogmatic temper. It leads the man of honor to scorn a piety that speaks lightly of his own creed. Whatever pietism gains in depth of motives, is partially lost again by the unfitness and narrowness of the expression. Perfect conduct, pervaded by a profound spirit, rests not even as an ideal, with either tendency. The religious life cannot fully justify itself to men till it unites honor and piety in manhood, good-will and reverence in righteousness; till its path forward is defined by a thorough redemption of the present hour. A life that is losing itself in its own pleasures, and one which lightens the labors of to-day only with the promise of to-morrow, are alike distasteful. A life that deepens and widens itself every moment, that is gaining authority, that is visibly beautiful and waiting on more prolific beauty, can alone call out the sustained enthusiasm of the soul. Let the beauty of the Lord our God be upon us.

The sources of piety and the sources of intellectual strength, the sources of religion and the sources of art, have tended to separation in the world's history. The humanist and the pietist have stood at opposite extremes. There has been much in the development of religious character that has been repulsive. The Christian has been as a patient who wears his plasters and swathing bands visibly about him, keeps an exact inventory of his ills, and fills the air with the odor of his diseases.

Grecian art and intellectuality were accompanied with relatively light religious sentiments. While we may thoroughly understand that the vital forces in historic life were flowing in the deep, narrow channels of faith rather than in those of art, that such a cañon as that of Puritanism held the sweet streams that were to refresh the garden of God, we may still feel that these cold waters must be softened by much sunshine before they can quicken all living things. We may find new emphasis in the prayer, Let the beauty of the Lord our God be upon us.

For a long time art found admission with difficulty into the Christian Church, and when it did enter it missed, as in painting, that vigor in the sensuous terms of life which art must always covet. The Last Sacrament of St. Jerome is so spiritualized off the plane of the senses as to give but an uncertain hold to art, art that handles the world, as God handles it, in and by the perfect image of itself. There was a constant conflict in Christian art, as it gathered strength, between classical and religious subjects; and the two terms were never reconciled, because neither faith nor art had risen to the point of union. Our piety should be like the box of precious ointment broken on the feet of Christ, filling the entire house with its grateful odor. Nor would Christ suffer any censure to fall on the act, though it seemed so far to transcend the close maxims of religious economy.

The power to penetrate the perfected forms of life with the true vigor of life, or, better, to express the vigor of life under its purified forms, is the real office of faith, and pietism intermeddles with it in this its divine mission. Pietism is to be corrected point by point, to be slowly widened in temper, saving at each transition its spirit of consecration by redirecting it into more comprehensive and rational forms of expression. The laws of life wait to be announced and enforced in all their manifold terms. We have no occasion to save our precious things that we may drop them later, one by one, in the endless stream of poverty and vice. We may lavish them at once in the service of the Master with a prodigality of faith far more effective than its parsimony, with a largeness of salvation preferable to every redemptive device, however just in itself. It is large ways not little ones that are to knit together the world in strength. The last passage of life is always union with the world, not separation from it; is setting all things at their divine service under the mind of God. What we need to occupy ourselves with is the wide mastery of truth, its universal redemptive power. Our purpose is not so much to crowd and huddle the fugitives of the world into the Church, as a place of immediate safety, as it is to march a conquering Church into the world for its instant renovation. The community is the larger of the two ideas. Not till the Church is co-extensive with the community will it be continuous with its own blessings.

CHAPTER V.

SPIRITUALISM.

The word spiritualism has sunk so ignominiously by association with the bastard idea of spiritism as to require a new consecration for any high calling. We mean by it the predominance of those incentives which are addressed to us through our spiritual nature, the fulness of that rational life which judges all things by their relation to righteousness, the rectitude of the soul itself.

The constitution of the human mind is such that it is able to take on a later and higher growth. Without this growth it is in conflict with itself, its efforts are abortive, and both the motives and the means of advancement slowly slip from it. With spiritual growth its purposes become more comprehensive, its resources more abundant, its satisfaction in its work more complete, and the subordination of conflicting tendencies more manifest. It is a simple psychological fact, involved in our original makeup, that the aims of life must be continually thrown forward, or life loses its dignity and fitness, and begins, in brief periods, to perish within itself. Spiritualism, or the supremacy of the higher and purer activities over the lower and grosser ones, is the normal unfolding of the mind of man. Without it life fails to become truly rational, and rapidly falls off from its possibilities.

The appetites and passions of men, in connection with

their power to anticipate the future and provide for it, call forth the desires, and the desires become the steady incentives to a large circle of activities and sensibilities that are self-seeking. The refinements of civilization rest chiefly on this basis of desire, intensified by the large development of social life. There is another circle of ideas which men win more slowly, and in connection with which the affections, the disinterested feelings, are unfolded. The three great lines of distinction, each capable within itself of the most varied development, are the true, the beautiful, and the good. If these are so united as to enlarge and correct each other, a new movement of life, a fresh network of relations, are brought forward for the profound modification of character. This form of activity is sustained by the affections; the entire line of development is lifted and becomes spiritual. New ends are established, and new principles of proportion rule conduct. This is a result distinctly provided for in the original powers of mind and in the growth of society. If it fails of fulfilment, the mind loses impulse and its resources drop off. There is a demand within the mind itself for this transfer of centre. The empirical philosophy expresses the change in a different phraseology, but it recognizes it and magnifies it. With this philosophy it is the repression of self-seeking tendencies and the cultivation of altruistic sentiments. The fundamental fact remains, however, though the method of conceiving it is diverse. Life becomes narrow, stagnant, poisonous, which does not constantly renew itself along its many flowing channels. It is a dead sea, made heavy and bitter by its own processes of evaporation. The mind relaxes its hold on spiritual relations, and tightens it on physical ones; and the more as these lose their power to bless it. The pessimism of exacting desires, unable to quell their own hunger, is a foregone conclusion.

It is in this field, cultivated by the lower sensibilities, that the higher insights enter. Character is sturdy, thrifty, and beautiful in the measure in which it gives expression, in these sensuous terms, to purer incentives. A truth that carries its harmony into the relations of society, a beauty that asserts itself in conduct, a righteousness that rectifies life in both its inner and outer lines of movement, provide separately and collectively a feast at which the soul can sit without weariness.

Precisely the same need arises in society as in the individual. Society is constantly reaching a stage in progress which it cannot make, a step in ascent it cannot surmount. Its resources are more abundant than ever before, its powers are on the increase, yet division and disintegration, extreme wealth and extreme poverty, are more manifest, and the general and permanent prosperity, for which so much has been undergone, is missed, just as men are reaching it. Discontent prevails, and counsel is taken for strife and overthrow rather than for new modes of advance. Why is this? Simply because men will not be spiritualized, because they carry animalism into a region beyond itself that it cannot cover. Under these conditions poverty and wealth alike vitiate the mind, enhance selfishness, and narrow tendencies already too restricted. Society becomes like an endogenous plant that is strangled by its own processes. Hardness and inflexibility are on the increase. Each new deposit is forced into position with greater and greater stress. Outward enlargement is arrested, and there is no further room for inward growth. The energy of life is consumed in resisting itself.

There is only one possible remedy for this suspension of social growth, spiritualism, a new harmony of feelings and actions on a higher plane, the substitution of prosperity expressed in terms of the affections for prosperity measured by the desires and translatable into a cash account. The moment men can find, truly find, their own good in the common good, their own joy in the enriched affections of all, they will have conquered life and discovered the conditions of social progress. When the poor are not blessed by the blessings of the rich, they think themselves impoverished by them; they certainly are spiritually impoverished by them, and fall into that remediless want—an envious, resentful, peevish temper. If the rich are not tried by the trials of the poor, they think themselves happily rid of them. But in shaking them off they have shaken off all divine tenderness, all breadth of emotional response, all lingering by the watercourses of life, and are leaving to dry up and wither those delicate fibres, that network of succulent tissue, by which the spiritually disposed incorporate themselves with the world, and feed upon it in its entire range of joy. The rich man may wonder that his pleasures are worth so little, fleeing so rapidly, and followed by so many dreary compensations. He may try to renew them by deepening the vicious taint in them; he may test the worth of the sensibility that he is wasting by wasting it still more rapidly. There can be but one result, darkness, made more overwhelming by a frenzied effort to dispel it. On this plane of desire there is but one wisdom, the wisdom of economy—slow, measured expenditure and sufficient stolidity to bear the inevitable.

The poverty of the selfishly rich and the selfishly poor in all life-giving pleasures ought not to surprise us. Life is a thing of wide, concurrent action, and is successful according to the extent and harmony of that action. Both are rejecting, over wide fields, the contributions of men and of society to human happiness, and putting in their place partial, divisive, and conflicting passions. Both are refusing the only real possible birth of higher life—that of spiritualism, aims that are as wide as truth, as assured as righteousness, as comprehensive as beauty. These aims, sustained in their pursuit at every step by the affections, can renovate society and make it a living whole whose experiences of pleasure and sorrow penetrate it in all its parts. History confirms, sociology enforces, the necessity of this transition in the centres of action and feeling in each man and among men. It is provided for in our constitution and is being made by insensible stages of growth. It is also one that can be accelerated by the push and elasticity of voluntary powers, and the spiritualizing vigor of truth in the free and open mind. It is to this last result that all the energies of devout men are directed. What we wish to point out more distinctly is that what we have now defined, hastily and inadequately, as a spiritualizing process, a pushing of life into its own proper field, is the work of Christ, his own conception of that work, the very sum and substance of that which is wrought by his love.

The words of Christ, comprehensively rendered, do not readily accept any other interpretation. This is their inner force and outer import. It is quite admissible to use some fulness of proof in establishing a point so easily lost sight of as this. It is essential when a deep current of obscure convictions has for a long time concealed the truth, and left it but partially operative; when the predominance of supernaturalism in men's thoughts has led them to look for quite other lessons, and reluctantly to accept the wise and patient ways of God; when carefully and artificially elaborated dogma and sporadic piety have helped to hide the paths of progress, to emphasize anew the first terms in spiritual life, and revive, in their primitive force, the words of Christ, as he leads us forward toward God. We believe that the teachings of Christ tend simply and directly to carry us onward in this spiritual development planted in the nature of man, and in the entire growth of society; and this lesson we desire to enforce. The whole movement, indeed, centres in God, in whom all truth, beauty, righteousness are gathered up in personal, emotional power; but this fact only defines the form of the enforcement, and does not alter the very nature of the transition.

Christ explicitly declares: "This is life eternal that they might know thee the only true God, and Jesus Christ whom thou hast sent."[1] Life eternal is spiritual knowledge. His declaration to the woman of Samaria bears the same import: "Whosoever drinketh of the water that I shall give him shall never thirst; but the water that I shall give him shall be in him a well of water springing up into everlasting life."[2] He gave the same truth a wider proclamation on the great day of the feast: "If any man thirst, let him come unto me and drink. He that believeth on me, as the Scripture hath said, out of his belly shall flow rivers of living water."[3]

Not unlike in force was the very different image addressed to Nicodemus: "Except a man be born again, he cannot see the kingdom of God."[4] Birth stands for a higher phase of life, one disunited from a lower life; and

---

[1] John xvii., 3.
[2] John iv., 14.
[3] John vii., 37.
[4] John iii., 3.

this higher life is born of water and spirit, of a purified and deepened experience. This is made plainer by the emphatic assertion : " Verily, verily I say unto you, He that heareth my word, and believeth in him that sent me hath everlasting life . . . He is passed from death unto life."[1] Everlasting life is not the reward of insight; it is involved in the insight itself. Thus, in Luke, it is affirmed : "The kingdom of God is within you"[2]; and in Mark: "Have salt within yourselves, and have peace one with another."[3]

This inner life, in its own distinctness, is to have its own line of development. New wine is to be put into new bottles and both are to be preserved.

There is no more perfect image of inner illumination than light. This is a favorite enforcement of Christ. He says of himself : "I am the light of the world."[4] Again: "I am the light of the world, he that followeth me shall not walk in darkness, but shall have the light of life."[5] So the apostle John opens his gospel with the declaration : "In him was life and the life was the light of men."[6] "That was the true light which lighteth every man that cometh into the world."[7] But light is in perfect fellowship with our powers. In the spiritual world we receive it and reflect it, "Ye are the light of the world." "Let your light so shine before men that they may see your good works and glorify your Father which is in heaven."[8] On the purity of this light personal well-being depends. "The light of the body is the eye; if, therefore, thine eye be single, thy whole body shall be full of light. But if

[1] John v., 24.
[2] Luke xvii., 21.
[3] Mark ix., 50.
[4] John ix., 5.
[5] John viii., 12.
[6] John i., 4.
[7] John i., 9.
[8] Matt. v., 16.

thine eye be evil, thy whole body shall be full of darkness. If, therefore, the light that is in thee be darkness, how great is that darkness!"[1]

That which specifically corresponds in the spiritual world to light is truth. Christ is the way, the truth, and the life. The spirit of God is the spirit of truth, that guides us into all truth. Our freedom is won by the truth: "Ye shall know the truth, and the truth shall make you free."[2] Sanctity arises in reception of the truth: "Sanctify them through the truth, thy word is truth."[3] What more explicit or more comprehensive or more glowing statement could be given of our relation to God than this; it is sharing with him the light and freedom of the truth.

But there remains another image which is hardly an image, it so touches the very substance of things. Life, that intangible something which stirs so potently among sensuous facts, and at the same time lies at the very centre of spiritual ones, seems, above all conceptions, to indicate the invisible pathway of thought by which we penetrate into the region of divine things. This is the supreme image on which Christ is ever laying the burden of his message. Life and death, lying at the lower and nearer end of this scale of organic being, illustrate and define life and death at the higher and farther extremity. Life is the expansion of power, death its overthrow. Holiness is rising into life, sin is sinking into death. The resources of life are gathered in Christ. "In him was life"; and to share his spirit is to enter into this life. "The hour is coming, and now is when the dead shall hear the voice of the Son of God, and they that hear shall live."[4] To miss

[1] Matt. vi., 22.
[2] John viii., 32.
[3] John xvii., 17.
[4] John v., 24.

his life by unbelief is to pass into the condemnation of death. We live and move and have our being in God. "Because I live ye shall live also,"[1] says Christ. "He that eateth me, even he shall live by me."[2] The dead hear the voice of the Son of God, and live. God is not a God of the dead, but of the living. "He that believeth in me, though he were dead, yet shall he live."[3] "Verily, verily, I say unto you, If a man keep my saying, he shall never see death."[4] "He that believeth not the Son, shall not see life."[5] "Ye will not come to me that ye might have life."[6] "I am the bread of life."[7] "I am the living bread which came down from heaven; if any man eat of this bread, he shall live forever."[8] "I am the resurrection and the life."[9] We are to understand these words of Christ in a profound way. The very substance of spiritual life, that on which it feeds, and the power by which it feeds, are held in the life of God, the life of truth which we share with him. To draw forth and bring forward this life is the work of Christ; and this life, as the highest term in life, rules all life. We live by it, and we perish without it. All casements give admission to this light of life.

This insight involves a transfer of the centre of activity upward. The intentions and affections and the profounder thoughts which sustain them must take the place of the appetites and passions and desires, and the sagacity which is developed in connection with them. This is repeatedly affirmed by Christ, and has justly been termed the secret of Christ. This subjection of the entire life to the higher laws which spring up in apprehension of the

[1] John xiv., 19. [4] John viii., 51. [7] John vi., 48.
[2] John vi., 57. [5] John iii., 36. [8] John vi., 51.
[3] John xi., 25. [6] John v., 40. [9] John xi., 25.

true, the beautiful, the good; this growth of all life out of these deeper impulses, this is the mind of Christ. "If any man will come after me, let him deny himself and take up his cross and follow me. For whosoever will save his life shall lose it; and whosoever will lose his life for my sake shall find it."[1] Life is here contrasted with itself, its lower with its higher forms. Life in its more immediate, sensuous expression must be repressed in favor of its more remote and spiritual development. Thus both forms of life are gained. Yielding to exorbitant desire, life is lost on both sides. The desires have no sufficient law and no adequate reward within themselves. They consume the life which they feed; they perish in their own excess. What can it profit a man if he win all the conditions of gratification—the whole world,—and sacrifice, in their pursuit, the only powers that can enable him to appropriate with real pleasure these gains? The affections are the assimilating organs of the soul; these lost, and all is lost. The eye with which we see is of more moment than the beauties of any one order offered to it. We can never wisely sacrifice a power in behalf of things addressed to that power. The insubordinate action of inferior powers can never compensate us for the subordinate action of the same powers; much less for the activity of the higher powers they are displacing. We truly possess the world by our insights, and ownership without insights is the poverty of the spirit made conspicuous.

Christ often returns to this fundamental principle, and sustains it by allied truths.[2] "Take no thought for your life, what ye shall eat; neither for the body, what ye shall

---

[1] Matt. xvi., 24.
[2] Matt. x., 39; Mark viii., 35; Luke ix., 24; Luke xiv., 33; John xii., 15.

put on. The life is more than meat, and the body is more than raiment." [1] "He that hath, to him shall be given; and from him that hath not, shall be taken even that which he hath." [2] This is the law of growth. Life suppressed, perishes; life nourished, rapidly gains power. Our work must be done under this principle. The same truth is emphasized under another form. The growth of the Kingdom of Heaven is likened to seed that first yields the blade, then the ear, then the full corn in the ear. The entire question is one of life, and the changing centres of life. This is also shown in the subordination of the means of life to life itself. The Sabbath was made for man, and not man for the Sabbath. Hence also the emphasis laid by Christ on a teachable spirit. The child is the most perfect image of the receptive temper. "Suffer little children to come unto me, and forbid them not, for of such is the kingdom of God." [3]

Closely allied with a true readiness to receive, is readiness to give. He who is teachable is prepared to teach. "If any desire to be first, the same shall be last of all, and servant of all. And he took a child and set him in the midst of them; and when he had taken him in his arms, he said unto them, Whosoever shall receive one of such children in my name, receiveth me; and whosoever shall receive me, receiveth not me, but him that sent me." [4] The essential thing in the Kingdom of Heaven, which is also the essential thing in the soul's insight into life, is a cheerful submission to the moral conditions which enclose us, and mastery under them and by them.

When we look at the work of Christ as an effort to secure this second birth, this uplift of the centre of life,

---

[1] Luke xii., 22.
[2] Mark iv., 25; Luke xix., 26.
[3] Luke xviii., 16; Mark x., 14.
[4] Mark ix., 36; Mark x., 42.

we readily understand his strong language concerning wealth. It is penetrating, but neither unwise nor untimely. " How hardly shall they that have riches enter into the kingdom of God. For it is easier for a camel to go through a needle's eye than for a rich man to enter into the kingdom of God."[1] The desire for wealth is the most central and universal of the desires. It especially awakens the echoes of self-interest in every apartment of the thoughts. It stands for an intense life on the level of personal interests. This desire, therefore, may well receive the stroke of rebuke aimed at a narrow and mischievous type of manhood. Christ is never careful to make all the corrections of thought which the truth ultimately calls for. The immediate force of his words would be much reduced by such a method. When the primary principle is recognized, its qualifications come readily. He speaks of the pursuit of wealth as one might speak of appetite to those subject to it. It is something which must be conquered at all costs. It stands for the dominance of desire. The real contrast of the defective and the perfect form of life needs nowhere to be drawn more sharply or with a firmer hand than at this very point—the pursuit of wealth. The words of Christ, extreme as they seem to be, are perfectly wholesome. They owe their cogency to the great danger of destroying life by the means of life; to the universality and persistency of the error of submitting the soul to its first terms of expansion. To have qualified, then and there, these words of revelation, would have been to emasculate them.

The estimate that Christ put on the living processes of faith is also seen in the points of censure he makes against

[1] Luke xviii., 24; Luke xvi., 13; Luke xii., 20.

the Pharisees. "Now do ye, Pharisees, make clean the outside of the cup and the platter; but your inward part is full of ravening and wickedness. Ye fools, did not he that made that which is without, make that which is within, also? But rather give alms of such things as ye have; and behold all things are clean unto you. But, woe unto you, Pharisees! for ye tithe mint and rue, and all manner of herbs, and pass over judgment and the love of God: these ought ye to have done and not to leave the others undone."[1] "Beware of the leaven of the Pharisees, which is hypocrisy."[2] All turns, censure and praise alike, on the inner force of the life. Note the beatitudes in this particular. It is the spirit of peace, purity, mercy, and meekness, the heart that hungers after righteousness, that are blessed. The favor of Heaven descends like dew and rain on these virtues.

Thus far we have spoken of the nature of the transformation in the life of man sought for by Christ. We turn to the lines of duty laid upon the obedient as another expression of the same thing. These also look to that change of intellectual and emotional centre which we are trying to enforce. The two great commandments on which hang all the law and the prophets are: "Thou shalt love the Lord thy God with all thy heart, and with all thy soul, and with all thy mind. Thou shalt love thy neighbor as thyself."[3] Here certainly the attention is carried at once over to the affections and to love, the chief affection, as the fulfilling of life. These commandments are weakened in their force by regarding them simply as injunctions to be met at once. They are rather long lines of light, unending changes, which bear us into

---

[1] Luke xi., 39. [2] Luke xii., 1; Luke xx., 46.
[3] Matt. xxii., 37; Mark xii., 30.

the centre of the divine mind and the higher life under it. We are to grow into perfect love, and this leaves nothing more to be desired. We cannot direct the attention too steadily to these commands as holding the inner law of spiritual things. They easily enfold all forms of praiseworthy action. "Therefore, all things whatsoever ye would that men should do unto you, do ye even so unto them."[1] "Love your enemies; do good to them which hate you, bless them that curse you, and pray for them which despitefully use you."[2] Admirable as are these injunctions, they are only single off-shoots of the parent principle. Give us that principle, and these follow. Lay down these commands without the divine impulse of love to supply the spirit of obedience, and they perish almost at once.

There is the favorite injunction of Christ that especially indicates the complete consciousness with which the life of the spirit was permeated, in his estimate of it: "If any man have ears to hear let him hear"[3]; "Take heed, therefore, how ye hear."[4] All things are to proceed under clear, inner light. It is a pure, intellectual atmosphere that is to embrace and offer in their intrinsic beauty all the conditions of spiritual conduct. The soul maintains its poise within itself. The range of the life is indicated in both directions. It is to possess the entire heart; it is to spread over the entire world. It looks to the highest possible, personal attainments. We are to be perfect, even as our Father which is in heaven is perfect. And this gospel of salvation is to be preached to every creature. The pyramid is as broad as the earth, and rises as high as heaven. The tree of life grows by the river of

---

[1] Matt. vii., 12.
[2] Luke vi., 27, 35; Luke xiv., 13; Matt. v., 43.
[3] Mark vii., 16.
[4] Luke viii., 18.

life, yields its fruits perpetually, and, with its leaves, heals the nations.

A most significant thing in this higher life, enjoined upon us, is its relation to God, the support it finds in him, and its relation to man, its nourishment under surrounding spiritual conditions. Both serve to define its nature. The relation in life that interprets to us all that is most tender, truthful, and noble is transferred to God. We find our way to him along a path cheered by every suggestion of consolation and help. We come to him as Our Father who art in heaven. All that is gathered up in parenthood, on its two sides of strength and love, is made to lighten the lines of approach to God. We abide in his presence under the most perfect form of love known to us, the fatherly and motherly affections which unfold with our own being, the sepals and petals which guard, nourish, and beautify the new-found life. This relationship is further presented to us in its most patient and benignant form in that gospel within a gospel, the parable of the prodigal son. The all-embracing impulse in the household of faith is that love of God granted unto us in the first commandment, the entire life drawn outward, upward tending, toward God. This carries with it the opening of the mind in insight into all spiritual things, the true, the beautiful, the good; and the springing up at once of those affections which are nourished by and nourish this spiritual unfolding of our powers.

The openness of this way is indicated in the parable of the publican, whose simple petition, God be merciful to me a sinner, swept aside every obstruction. It is enforced by the parable of the lost sheep, and the piece of silver that was lost. Man may not only return to God, he is diligently sought after by him: "There is joy in the presence of the angels of God over one sinner that repenteth." [1]

The spiritual character of our union with God is explicitly affirmed, and we are not allowed to search for it on any lower plane than that of inner life. "God is a spirit, and they that worship him must worship him in spirit and in truth." [2] "Of his fulness have all we received, and grace for grace." [3]

The part taken by Christ in this union of our thoughts with God is abundantly defined. As indicated in the passage last given, we are partakers in his fulness in lineal descent, virtue by virtue. No man cometh unto the Father but by him, because he is the truth and the life. He embraces them both. A variety of images are used which unfold this thought on all sides to the light. He is the door to the fold, and, in the same breath, its shepherd. He is the vine of which we are the branches, the bread of life on which we feed. This last image is amplified and put with a literalness that compels us to spiritualize it. "Verily, verily, I say unto you, except ye eat the flesh of the Son of Man, and drink his blood, ye have no life in you." [4] The crass character of the image cuts us off from any gross use of it. We make nothing of it, till we make everything of it, till it means for us the appropriation and assimilation of the life of Christ.

Thus are we led into the fellowship of God, and it is one of light and life and love. The Comforter that is sent unto us, that dwelleth in us forever, that takes of the things of Christ and shows them unto us, is the

[1] Luke xv., 10.
[2] John iv., 24; John i., 12.
[3] John i., 16.
[4] John vii., 153.

Spirit of Truth. All is love. "If a man love me he will keep my words, and my Father will love him, and we will come unto him and make our abode with him."[1] In whatever direction we turn, there is one spiritual presence, one revelation, one impulse. "When he, the Spirit of Truth, is come, he will guide you into all truth."[2] "As the Father hath loved me, so have I loved you; continue ye in my love. If ye keep my commandments, ye shall abide in my love; even as I have kept my Father's commandments and abide in his love."[3] "And now I am no more in the world, but these are in the world, and I come to thee. Holy Father, keep through thine own name those whom thou hast given me, that they may be one, as we are."[4] Nor is this any idle fellowship of unproductive sentiments in a mystical world of dreams. It is a fellowship of labor, suffering, conquest. "Ye shall, indeed, drink of the cup that I drink of; and with the baptism that I am baptized withal shall ye be baptized."[5] "Ye call me Master and Lord; and ye say well; for so I am. If I then, your Lord and Master, have washed your feet; ye ought also to wash one another's feet. For I have given you an example, that ye should do as I have done to you."[6] But this service has in it no element of bondage, it is wholly one of loving insight. "Henceforth I call you not servants; for the servant knoweth not what his Lord doeth; but I call you friends; for all things that I have heard of my Father I have made known unto you."[7]

This relation of man to God contains and implies his relation to his fellow-men; and any philosophy of life will

[1] John vi., 23.
[2] John xvi., 13.
[3] John xv., 9.
[4] John xviii., 11.
[5] John x., 39.
[6] John xiii., 13.
[7] John xv., 15.

meet with great difficulty in enforcing the fellowship of humanity that is not able to root it thoroughly in the very constitution of the spiritual world. Out of the abundant energy of the first command, the second command springs readily: Thou shalt love thy neighbor as thyself. Nor was Christ content to leave the injunction to the rendering of men. He defined the most essential term in it, and indicated the method of fulfilment in the beautiful parable of the good Samaritan. The injunction of love is not left by Christ as a general principle simply. He returns to it constantly, with much tenderness, as the true bond between his disciples. As the conditions of discipleship give free play to the affections, so should they knit all together in one vigorous fellowship of love. "A new"—new in its vital force—"commandment I give unto you, That ye love one another; as I have loved you, that ye also love one another. By this shall all men know that ye are my disciples, if ye have love one for another."[1] "This is my commandment, That ye love one another, as I have loved you. Greater love hath no man than this, that a man lay down his life for his friend."[2] This love is to be no unfruitful affection. It is to find expression in every act of service from the least to the greatest, from a cup of cold water to the giving of life. Honor in this fraternity of Christ should be found in following in the steps of the Master. "Ye know that the princes of the Gentiles exercise dominion over them, and they that are great exercise authority upon them. But it shall not be so among you; but whosoever will be great among you, let him be your minister; and whosoever will be chief among you, let him be your servant; even as the Son of Man came not to be

[1] John xiii., 34.   [2] John xv., 12-15, 17.

ministered unto, but to minister, and to give his life a ransom for many."[1]

But this temper of kindly service is possible among men of grave faults and petty infirmities only in connection with forgiveness ; and Christ lays down the law of forgiveness in its most absolute form. There is to be in us a divine tenderness cherishing every germ of life. There is not only not the least trace of an implacable temper in Christ, there is no recognition of any principle of justice that stands in the way of forgiveness when forgiveness is sought. "How oft," inquires Peter, "shall my brother sin against me, and I forgive him? till seven times? Jesus saith unto him, I say not unto thee, Until seven times; but, Until seventy times seven."[2] This forgiveness is enjoined as being at one with the divine method. "And when ye stand praying, forgive, if ye have ought against any: that your Father also which is in heaven may forgive you your trespasses."[3] No words certainly can express more explicitly and in more varied directions than do these words of Christ that the thing sought by him was a new centre of life, planted in the affections of men.

We have striven to show how Christ defines this change in itself, the lines of duty which he lays down in connection with it, the relations which men sustain by it to God and to their fellow-men. Its nature is also involved in the tests given us by which we are to judge whether this transfer of life has been effected. They are of the simplest and plainest order. Every good tree is to bring forth good fruit. As Bacon felt that all knowledge should be fruitful, so Christ would have all righteousness beneficent. "A

---

[1] Matt. xx., 25. [2] Matt. xviii., 21 ; Luke xvii., 3.
[3] Mark xi., 24.

good man out of the good treasure of his heart bringeth forth that which is good."[1] Our kinship with Christ is one of well-doing. "My mother and my brethren are those which hear the word of God and do it."[2] When John the Baptist sought evidence of the Messiahship of Christ, Christ made answer, "Go your way, and tell John what things ye have seen and heard; how that the blind see, the lame walk, the lepers are cleansed, the deaf hear, the dead are raised, to the poor the Gospel is preached."[3]

The censures of Christ involve the same criterion, "Go ye and learn what that meaneth, I will have mercy and not sacrifice; for I am not come to call the righteous, but sinners to repentance."[4] "Those things which proceed out of the mouth come forth from the heart; and they defile the man."[5] There is nothing which drew so severe a rebuke from Christ as a disposition to substitute traditions and rites for large obedience. "Laying aside the commandment of God, ye hold the tradition of men, as the washing of pots and cups: and many other such things ye do."[6] "Woe unto you, scribes and Pharisees, hypocrites! for ye pay tithe of mint, and anise and cummin, and have omitted the weightier matters of the law—judgment, mercy, and faith; these ought ye to have done and not to leave the other undone. Ye blind guides, which strain at a gnat, and swallow a camel."[7] The obedience of Christ proceeds in full knowledge. Blessed are your eyes, for they see; and your ears, for they hear. The scribe, taught in the things of the Kingdom of Heaven, is versa-

---

[1] Luke vi., 45; xiii., 9: viii., 15.
[2] Luke viii., 21.
[3] Luke vii., 22.
[4] Matt. ix., 13.
[5] Matt. xv., 18.
[6] Mark vii., 8.
[7] Matt. xxiii., 23.

tile in their use, and brings forth the new and the old as occasion calls for them.

This life of the spirit leads one to put away all asceticism. Christ came eating and drinking. Soundness of mind and soundness of body are ultimately identical. " For whether is easier, to say, Thy sins be forgiven thee; or to say, Arise, and walk."[1]

A method like this of Christ is applicable to all men under all circumstances, and so has found admission aside from his presence. " Many shall come from the east and the west, and shall sit down with Abraham, and Isaac, and Jacob, in the Kingdom of Heaven."[2] "Other sheep, I have, which are not of this fold: them also I must bring, and they shall hear my voice; and there shall be one fold and one shepherd."[3] This divine grace proceeds always under the one ethical law, " Unto whomsoever much is given, of him shall much be required."[4]

It is not easy to overestimate the concurrent and accumulated force of these words of Christ. They all look, from every variety of position, toward a life built up within itself, according to its own constitution, into strength, and so into the grace of God. God gives to those who have. Nor are there any passages in the Gospels that cast any other light on the subject. There are a few, taken by themselves, as " He that believeth and is baptized shall be saved,"[5] which might perplex us, but, in the general blaze of light, they also reflect the spirituality of the things about them. No precept in the Gospels enforces a dogma or a rite as in itself a duty. All rests on the basis of naturalism, the constitution of man,

---

[1] Matt. ix., 5.
[2] Matt. viii., 11; Luke xiii., 29.
[3] John x., 16.
[4] Luke xiv., 48.
[5] Mark xvi., 16.

of society, and of the Kingdom of Heaven. Beliefs and duties are grounded in their spiritual occasions, and enforced by them.

Even more weight than has been laid may well be laid on the method of instruction by Christ. It is by illustrations, by parables, by facts of experience. The general statement, when it comes, rests back on examples. Many things are gained by this manner of expounding recondite truth. The disciples were not allowed to put their own facile interpretations on the words of Christ, and to suppose that they understood them, when they had but begun to penetrate them. This has been a great difficulty in religious instruction; a superficial, conventional sentiment has come to incrust the words in which it is uttered, and to hide from the eye the germs of truth they contain. The disciples were put to their wit's end by the words of Christ, and were disposed to complain of the obscurity of his parables. If we mean by clearness of expression the power to convey ideas, then the instructions of Christ were most lucid. Ways which would have seemed plainer to the disciples would have hidden from them the burden of the message. Awakened attention was the first condition of apprehension.

This method gave also an inductive basis to the discourses of Christ, which quite distinguishes them from current religious methods, magnifying their own verbal distinctions, and leaving wholly behind them empirical facts. Thus when Christ justified healing on the Sabbath by the argument: "Doth not each one of you on the sabbath loose his ox or his ass from the stall, and lead him away to watering? And ought not this woman, being a daughter of Abraham, whom Satan hath bound, lo, these eighteen years, be loosed from this bond on the sabbath day?"[1] he was introducing a new method of looking at religious truth, and one which grew directly out of the facts of life.

The parable was fitted to make the impression that the world, in all its details, was full of the divine mind; full of lessons designed to put us in living interchange of truth with it. The remoteness and unreality which attach to spiritual things were dispelled, and the physical form and spiritual force of events were set at one again.

This figurative method of Christ compelled the disciples to break step, to take long strides and great leaps in catching up with the truth; to overlook superficial agreements, and seek after the profound, the real, points at which the assertion and the illustration, the principle and its image, coalesce. A lazy interpretation of the parables without penetration lands one in absurdities, and the truth must be kept aloof from the illustration at the same time that it is reflected by it. The image in the mirror is not more distinct from the mirror itself than is the very truth from the things which unfold it.

For this reason, because the right rendering turns on penetrative insight, the image has wonderful power to preserve the truth and to transmit it, beyond the reach of conventional perversions, from person to person and period to period. That we save our lives by sacrificing them is a riddle which each man must expound successfully from the secrets of his own soul. The astute dialectician finds difficulty in subjecting truth, put in this form, to his barren processes. He must translate it into dogma before he can ply it with inferences, and lead it on and on, far from the corrections of experience and the government of life. The words of Christ are full of an emotional ele-

[1] Luke xiii., 15.

ment, are penetrated by living terms, which make it difficult to turn them into abstractions.

The liberty of the disciple is thus fully preserved. There is a direct appeal to his own mind and heart, which brings the problem of life home to him for his personal solution. The thoughts are brought near the truth and left alone with it as by the words of no other teacher.

We shall not understand what Christ aims to do for men, the transformation he desires to work in them, till we understand what he himself was. It is his own life, his estimate of truth, that are the conquering powers of the spiritual world. Christ was a presentation of pure and patient love as a ruling force in the human soul. On this basis he built his life, under this idea he ripened it to its end. The love here opened for our admiration is a rational affection; a feeling that runs along the lines of truth and makes them rivers of life; a sentiment that clings, with unwavering insight, to the law of righteousness as the upward tending strength of the growing spirit; an emotion that breaks forth in scorching rebuke of sin, because it would purge the soil as by fire of the brambles and thorns which hold it from the uses of men. Principles and precepts were in the world prior to Christ, the fitting forms of life were more or less present to the imagination of men, but the divine force was hardly awakened in the soul by which these principles were to receive power, these forms be fulfilled in living things. Christ made it manifest that there were fountains of affection deep enough in God and in man—in man because in God—to thoroughly refresh and fertilize the world. He wrought out the problem of life on the practical side. Henceforth it became in order to exhort men, Be not overcome of evil, but overcome evil with good.

The entire struggle of Christ, his bearing our infirmities and carrying our sins, is found in this confronting within his own spirit of every error and sin, and putting them aside with a new assertion of truth and love—truth that stands for love, and love that stands for truth. The bruised reed was not broken, the smoking flax was not quenched, his voice was not heard in the street. One remedy, one only and one always, was with him, a deeper assertion of the divine life of the soul. If I be lifted up, I will draw all men unto me. If this victory of love, binding the soul to God and to men in holiness, is made complete in me, it shall be the victory of all time. Those night watches upon the mountains were the bracing up of the spirit within itself, as it held fast to its purpose; the conquering power of spiritual purity; the giving of all, and so the winning of all. The transfiguration followed one of these struggles in which the soul wrestled successfully—clinging to the redemptive grace of God—against all the discouragements, disappointments, delays, passions, perversities, follies and foolish rhapsodies, that penetrate the atmosphere of the world, like heat and cold, and make it a bitter place for tender, pure, and loving spirits. The transfiguration was a visible expression of a transmutation which this unquenchable love shall make universal. When Christ, having turned aside not one moment from the simple declaration of truth, having yielded nothing and precipitated nothing in the conflict of sin with holiness, hatred with love, was able, on the cross—a defeat of grace from which all spiritual victories take their date, a victory of transgression from which the growing overthrow of evil is ever proceeding—to say, Father forgive them, they know not what they do, he was also able to add, It is finished, into thy hands I commit my spirit.

All is one, the life of Christ, the work of Christ, the salvation of men—the soul knit together within itself in pure affections, the life transferred to its eternal centre in God.

The one thing which explains the world in its confusion, suffering, and darkness is growth—movement forward into order, life, light. This growth is at once most comprehensive and most special, most extensive and most minute. It aims at the perfection of the individual as the condition of perfect society, while society draws into its development from above and below all spiritual and physical resources. This growth of man involves a rhythmic pulsation that extends through and through the world of which he is a portion. Motion is a most exhilarating physical experience. Motion upward, motion that diffuses itself broadly, is, in its sense of concurrent and sympathetic power, the most animating form of motion. Growth, such growth as that of which we are now speaking, involves the most extended, concurrent, upward movement; one of which physical motion is but a feeble image. He who feels it, sees its conditions, experiences its delight, catches sight of its implications, can scarcely make any question as to the worth of life, or the wisdom with which it is ordered. The discouragements of the moment are revealed only by the light which lies before us; the ills that are about us are the incentives to the good that is to displace them. The sense of confusion arises from the scope of the movement which encloses us, and its delay from the magnitude of the field it is covering. We are oppressed with the weight of immeasurable things, but only thus have we the sweep of immortality. We miss the pleasures that are near us, but only because we have not yet learned how best to appropriate all pleasure. We mistake many things and pervert many, because this growth is of our very substance, must be self-achieved and slowly permeated by the light of our own consciousness. We are held back by the faults and failures and sins of others only because our supreme profiting lies in the fulfilments and virtues of all men, because we harvest not one pitiful field set apart as our own, but the whole world; because love—the love of wisdom and the wisdom of love—pulsating with the stroke of spiritual health through all rational life, throbs sympathetically in our veins, and takes its measure in us from the impulse of the divine mind, seeking for itself the Kingdom of Heaven.

We meet with difficulty in grasping this idea of growth, because, by a strange perversion of ideas, things seem to us coherent, involved in each other in all ways, while acts, personal efforts, seem isolated, capable of sudden throes of power and quick upheavals of creative energy. It is thought that is, of its own nature, thoroughly and forever coherent. Intellectual, spiritual creations must be traversible in all directions along all lines of connection. The cement of things is thought, but thought itself is struck through with rational order in every movement. Failing of this it ceases to be thought. Incoherent progress in the spiritual world, a transformation not known to itself, is self-contradictory. Things may be built together,—they have grown together that they might be in closer sympathy with mind—thoughts, spiritual affections, cannot be built together. They must in every stage of progress pass up into the light by their own movement. The spiritual pace of the universe is all that we can bear. We are gathered up as rapidly as we are able into the rational movement of the divine mind.

This fact felt, and so accepted, and there is the same open vision and delightful mystery in the progress of the world that there is in the fragrant summer dawn as it breaks into day. We wish not to hasten the glorious disclosure. There is too much in each moment to allow us to be impatient for the next. It is the child, not the man, that deals so obscurely and weakly with what he has as to turn hope into the fret of weariness, and to make pleasure yield only a desire for the next enjoyment in order. Peace, rest in motion, the power to pursue good, this is the divine gift, not to be given but to be won.

In this growth we need a naturalism which makes our entire path coherent, interlaced each moment with one rational movement; we need a supernaturalism which nourishes our sense of power, and puts us in conscious fellowship with the Supreme Power that rules the current of events on which we are borne. These are the conditions and the motives of our spiritual manhood. We must also understand that conventional forms of thought and conventional forms of religious action, dogmatism and pietism, are only provisional, are to be constantly reshaped by more penetrative and more comprehensive vision, as we move forward in personal and social attainment, as we develop the spiritual life that takes to itself, and harmonizes within itself, all life. We must attain that spiritualism, which sees all things, understands them all, and enjoys them all, from that centre of reason which rests in the Divine Mind.

The New Theology is not then new, but as old as the world in the inner force which brings it forward. It indicates, indeed, a productive spring-tide of thought, but its seeds are those of many previous seasons. It is one more movement, standing in file with a thousand others past and to come, by which the limitations of knowledge give way, and we are enabled to take another step upward in the revelation of God, another step forward in the largeness of the gospel of Christ.

Naturalism becomes to us, as it does to all true science, the continuity, the omnipresence, of the divine method; supernaturalism becomes to us, as it does to all reverent, loving faith, the inner force of the natural, unfolding in visible forms the invisible things of the spirit. We are patient with dogma, because many men are standing upon it, and we too in our own way; we are thankful for pietism, because even in its more spasmodic moods it is still an experience and expression of life. But we wait on the efforts and aspirations of all good men, as they accumulate the conditions of that sound and pervasive spirituality which is to unite the earth under us and the heavens over us, according to the mind of God, into the Kingdom of Heaven. Thus is nothing destroyed, but all things are fulfilled.

The individual life can only express itself in terms of the common life, for this is the field of the affections; the common life can only disclose its wealth in the wealth of the individual, for the individual is the unit in all its enumerations. Each waits on all, and all wait on each. Love reveals itself to love alone. The future is obscure to us, because we have not yet reached the spiritual points of overlook. We move forward under a wide naturalism, implanted in our own constitution, the constitution of society, and in the Divine Mind. This maps for us the otherwise unexplored path. The desire reverently and obediently to wait on each fresh revelation in this upward-tending way is the temper of the New Theology.

It breaks only with that scheme of theology which so interpenetrates our relations to God with supernaturalism as to obscure for us human character, the laws of spiritual growth, the grace of Christ, and the meaning of salvation.

THE END

PUBLICATIONS OF G. P. PUTNAM'S SONS.

WORKS BEARING ON THE STUDY OF THE BIBLE.

I. **The Bible of To-Day.** By JOHN W. CHADWICK. 8vo, cloth extra $1 50

"The need of some such work is keenly felt by thousands of intelligent persons who are not in a position to make an adequate study of the elaborate works in which this criticism has written its comments, yet earnestly desire to know what conclusions the various scholars who have made studies of the subject have reached."—*N. Y. Evening Post.*

II. **The Bible. What is it?** An attempt briefly to answer the question in the light of the best scholarship, and in the most reverent and catholic spirit. By the Rev. J. T. SUNDERLAND. 16mo, cloth 1 00

"His criticisms are scholarly, thorough, and uncompromising, but he leaves ample room for a powerful defence of the Bible in its spiritual aspects as the unfailing depository of religious faith and moral inspiration."—*N. Y. Tribune.*

III. **Benedicite; or, Illustrations of the Power, Wisdom, and Goodness of God, as Manifested in his Works.** By G. CHAPLIN CHILD, M.D. With an Introduction by HENRY G. WESTON, D.D. 12mo, cloth extra, beveled 2 00

"A most admirable popular treatise of natural theology. It is no extravagance to say that we have never read a more charming book, or one that we can recommend more confidently to our readers with the assurance that it will aid them, as none that we know of can do, to

"'Look through Nature up to Nature's God.'"—*Round Table*, N. Y.

V **The Book of the Beginnings.** A study of Genesis, with a general introduction to the study of the Pentateuch. By Rev. R. HEBER NEWTON.
16mo, cloth, pp. xv.+307 . . . . . 1 00
Paper 40

"These 'talks' will be acceptable to the general public, who wish to see on what grounds the critics base their conclusions respecting the Pentateuch."—*The Nation.*

VI. **The Right and Wrong Uses of the Bible.** By Rev. R. HEBER NEWTON. 16mo, cloth, pp. 264 . 75

"It is impossible to read these sermons without high admiration of the author's courage, of his honesty, his reverential spirit, his wide and careful reading, and his true conservatism."—*American Literary Churchman.*

G. P. PUTNAM'S SONS   NEW YORK AND LONDON.

IMPORTANT RELIGIOUS WORKS.

Gospel-Criticism and Historical Christianity. A study of the Gospels and of the History of the Gospel Canon during the Second Century ; together with a consideration of the results of Modern Criticism. By Orello Cone, D.D. 8vo, cloth, gilt top $1 75

"The book is rich in material and is a good example of the proper study of Gospel literature."—*Public Opinion*, Washington, D. C.

The Religion of Humanity. By O. B. Frothingham. 4th edition, 12mo, pp. 338 . . . . $1 50

"A profoundly sincere book, the work of one who has read largely, studied thoroughly, reflected patiently."—*Boston Globe*.

Stories from the Lips of the Teacher. By O. B. Frothingham. Retold by a Disciple. Sixth edition, 16mo, pp. 193 . $1 00

"It is in style and thought a superior book, that will interest young and old."—*Zion Herald* (Methodist).

Stories of the Patriarchs. By O. B. Frothingham. Third edition, 16mo, pp. 232 . . . . $1 00

"The sublimest lessons of manhood in the simple language of a child." *Springfield Republican*.

The Child's Book of Religion. By O. B. Frothingham. For Sunday-Schools and Homes. New edition, revised. 16mo, pp. xii. + 273 . . . . $1 00

Transcendentalism in New England. By O. B. Frothingham. A History. Second edition. 8vo, pp. iv. + 394 . . $1 75

"The book is masterly and satisfying."—*Appleton's Journal*.

The Cradle of the Christ. By O. B. Frothingham. A Study in Primitive Christianity. 8vo, pp. x. + 234 . . . $1 50

"Scholarly, acute, and vigorous."—*N. Y. Tribune*.

Theodore Parker. By O. B. Frothingham. A Biography. 8vo, pp. viii. + 588 . . . . $2 00

Gerrit Smith. By O. B. Frothingham. A Biography. 8vo, pp. 371 . . . . $2 00

"A good biography, it is faithful, sufficiently full, written with vigor, grace, and good taste." *N. Y. Evening Post*.

Belief of the Unbelievers. By O. B. Frothingham. 12mo, sewed 25

Speaking of Mr. Frothingham's Sermons, the *Springfield Republican* says: "No one of serious intellectual character can fail to be interested and taught by these most thoughtful discourses."

Boston Unitarianism. By O. B. Frothingham. 1820–1840. A Study of the Life and Work of Nathaniel Langdon Frothingham. 8vo, pp. 272 . . . . $1 75

"The book, to a thoughtful reader, cannot fail to be elevating and suggestive of high ideals, high thinking, and noble living."—*Newark Advertiser*.

Recollections and Impressions. By O. B. Frothingham. 1822–1890. 8vo $1 50

G. P. PUTNAM'S SONS, NEW YORK AND LONDON

PUBLICATIONS OF G. P. PUTNAM'S SONS

THE SCRIPTURES,

HEBREW AND CHRISTIAN.

ARRANGED AND EDITED AS AN INTRODUCTION TO THE STUDY OF THE BIBLE.

Rev. EDWARD T. BARTLETT, L.D.,
Dean of the Divinity School of the P. E. Church in Philadelphia, and Mary Wolfe, Prof. of Ecclesiastical History.

Rev. JOHN P. PETERS, Ph.D.,
Professor of Old Testament Literature and Language in the Divinity School of the P. E. Church in Philadelphia, and Professor of Hebrew in the University of Pennsylvania.

} EDITORS.

The work is to be completed in three volumes, containing each about 500 pages. Vols. I. and II. now ready.

Vol. I. includes Hebrew story from the Creation to the time of Nehemiah, as in the Hebrew canon.

Vol. II. is devoted to Hebrew poetry and prophecy.

Vol. III. will contain the selections from the Christian Scriptures.

The volumes are handsomely printed in 12mo form, and with an open, readable page, not arranged in verses, but paragraphed according to the ense of the narrative.

Each volume is complete in itself, and will be sold separately at $1.50.

The editors say in their announcement: "Our object is to remove stones of stumbling from the path of young readers by presenting Scriptures to them in a form as intelligible and as instructive as may be practicable. This plan involves some re-arrangements and omissions, before which we have not hesitated, inasmuch as our proposed work will not claim to be the Bible, but an introduction to it. That we may avoid imposing our own interpertation upon Holy Writ, it will be our endeavor to make Scripture serve as the commentary on Scripture. In the treatment of the Prophets of the Old Testament and the Epistles of the New Testament, it will not be practicable entirely to avoid comment, but no attempt will be made to pronounce upon doctrinal questions."

The first volume is divided into four parts:

PART I.—HEBREW STORY, FROM THE BEGINNING TO THE TIME OF SAUL.
" II.—THE KINGDOM OF ALL ISRAEL.
" III.—SAMARIA, OR THE NORTHERN KINGDOM.
" IV.—JUDAH, FROM REHOBOAM TO THE EXILE.

PUBLICATIONS OF G. P. PUTNAM'S SONS

The second volume comprises:

PART I.—HEBREW HISTORY FROM THE EXILE TO NEHEMIAH.
" II.—HEBREW LEGISLATION.
" III —HEBREW TALES.
" IV.—HEBREW PROPHECY.
" V.—HEBREW POETRY.
" VI.—HEBREW WISDOM.

The third volume will comprise the selections from the New Testament, arranged as follows:

I.—THE GOSPEL ACCORDING TO ST. MARK, PRESENTING THE EVANGELICAL STORY IN ITS SIMPLEST FORM; SUPPLEMENTED BY SELECTIONS FROM ST. MATTHEW AND ST. LUKE.
II.—THE ACTS OF THE APOSTLES, WITH SOME INDICATION OF THE PROBABLE PLACE OF THE EPISTLES IN THE NARRATIVE.
III.—THE EPISTLES OF ST. JAMES AND THE FIRST EPISTLE OF ST. PETER.
IV.—THE EPISTLES OF ST. PAUL.
V.—THE EPISTLE TO THE HEBREWS.
VI.—THE REVELATION OF ST. JOHN (A PORTION).
VII.—THE FIRST EPISTLE OF ST. JOHN.
VIII.—THE GOSPEL OF ST. JOHN.

Full details of the plan of the undertaking, and of the methods adopted by the editors in the selection and arrangement of the material, will be found in the separate prospectus.

"I congratulate you on the issue of a work which, I am sure, will find a wide welcome, and the excellent features of which make it of permanent value."—Rt. Rev. HENRY C. POTTER, Bishop of New York.

"Should prove a valuable adjunct of Biblical instruction."—Rt. Rev. W. E. STEVENS, Bishop of Pennsylvania.

"Admirably conceived and admirably executed. . . . It is the Bible story in Bible words. The work of scholarly and devout men. . . . Will prove a help to Bible study."—Rev. HOWARD CROSBY, D.D.

"We know of no volume which will better promote an intelligent understanding of the structure and substance of the Bible than this work, prepared, as it is, by competent and reverent Christian scholars."—*Sunday-School Times.*

G. P. PUTNAM'S SONS

NEW YORK:　　　　　　　　　　　　LONDON:
27 AND 29 WEST 23D STREET　　　27 KING WILLIAM ST., STRAND

www.ingramcontent.com/pod-product-compliance
Lightning Source LLC
Chambersburg PA
CBHW021820230426
43669CB00008B/817